CLOISTER

BOOKS

Cloister Books are inspired
by the monastic custom of
reading as one walks slowly
in the monastery cloister—
a place of silence, centering,
and calm. Within these pages
you will find a similar space
in which to pray and reflect
on the presence of God.

*C*OWLEY *PUBLICATIONS* is a ministry of the brothers of the Society of Saint John the Evangelist, a monastic order in the Episcopal Church. Our mission is to provide books and resources for those seeking spiritual and theological formation. Cowley Publications is committed to developing a new generation of writers and teachers who will encourage people to think and pray in new ways about spirituality, reconciliation, and the future.

Advance Praise for *Mass in Time of War*

Using the form and essence of the Mass, Barbara Crafton examines the complex questions and the inward struggles which we as individuals, and collectively as communities, have wrestled with since September 11, 2001. Her description of the restaurant Windows on the World in the World Trade Center is so graphic and poignant that the reader cannot but face the tragedy in one's own being. Profoundly, she points through the tragedy of the day to a future that will not be denied.

~ Edmond Browning, Presiding Bishop, *retired*

In this disturbing prophetic volume Barbara Crafton speaks hard truth to power and to all of us in the continuing aftermath of September 11, 2001. She does so in contemporary parlance, yet with the fiery intensity of an ancient Isaiah, Jeremiah or Amos and during a period in our nation's unfolding history— a time of war—when it not only is unpopular, but dangerous as well. While Crafton may lose some "patriotic" fans, she also will win some seekers after truth.

~ Barbara C. Harris, Bishop Suffragan,
Massachusetts, *retired*

Published in the United States of America by Cowley Publications, a division of the Society of Saint John the Evangelist. No portion of this book may be reproduced, stored in or introduced into a retrieval system, or transmitted, in any form or by any means—including photocopying—without the prior written permission of Cowley Publications, except in the case of brief quotations embedded in critical articles and reviews.

Library of Congress Cataloging-in-Publication Data:
Crafton, Barbara Cawthorne.
  Mass in time of war / Barbara Cawthorne Crafton.
      p. cm.
Includes bibliographical references.
  ISBN 1-56101-213-0 (pbk. : alk. paper)
  1. September 11 Terrorist Attacks, 2001—Religious aspects—Episcopal Church. I. Title.
  BT736.15.C725 2003
  242'.4--dc21

                            2003012914

Scripture quotations are taken from *The New Revised Standard Version* of the Bible, © 1989, by the Division of Christian Education of the National Council of the Churches of Christ in the United States of America. Used by permission.

Cover design: Gary Ragaglia

This book was printed by Transcontinental Printing in Canada on acid-free paper.

Cowley Publications
907 Massachusetts Avenue
Cambridge, Massachusetts 02139
800-225-1534 • www.cowleypublications.org

Mass in Time of War

For Parke –
Brother in Christ –

[signature]

Mass
of War
in Time

by
Barbara Cawthorne Crafton

Contents

This book is dedicated with respect and love to
Paul Moore, Thirteenth Bishop of New York, 1919–2003

United
States
Marine,
Priest, Bishop, Prophet,
Peacemaker To the end.
May his
soul, and
the souls
of all the
faithful
departed,
rest in peace.

Deliver us from the presumption
of coming to this Table for solace only,
and not for strength;
for pardon only,
and not for renewal.
~*The Book of Common Prayer* (1979),
Eucharistic Prayer C (p. 372)

i

Foreword

You are holding in your hands the text to a Mass, not a lamentation, and an unexpected kind of Mass at that. The anticipated requiem Mass has largely to do with rest for what is ended, but this Mass is no requiem—nothing is laid to rest. This Mass, a more agitated form, a Mass in time of war, is about unfinished business. Barbara Crafton moves, inspires, and instructs us as she takes up that business in her recollection of September 11, 2001 and its aftermath.

A few months ago the papers were full of the architect's proposals for new buildings at Ground Zero. They all included a memorial to the dead and the heroes of the 9/11 disaster, of course, but a decent interval has now passed, and we have begun to forget, to rebuild, to "get on with our lives," as the saying too often goes.

The autumn of 2001 was a time of revelation. We saw American heroes in action. We saw Americans bearing grief unlike anything they have wept over since the attack on Pearl Harbor. We saw compassion flower; its bloom transcends the otherness we usually impose on faces of any color unlike our own. We saw a lame duck mayor exercise leadership that everyone who aspires to serve the public should study and digest. We saw, perhaps for the first time, how variously America is perceived around the globe. To "get on with our lives" without carrying these and other revelations with us would be the final disaster of 9/11.

Those who here reflect with Mother Crafton will be spared that disaster. Her *Introit* gathers the distracted and the forgetful and makes us mindful and resolute. Each following movement of her Mass shows us the best and the worst of our species, and we are driven to ask about God for real this time as we move through the chants to the liturgy's abrupt and lifelike dismissal.

That movement is not an easy journey. The reflections found here will—with ruthless compassion—reopen wounds so that they can be cleaned and properly stitched, the edges aligned correctly. We will appreciate again much of what is best about America and pinpoint what is despicable about terrorism. However, if we accept it as more than a platitude—or a desecration—we will also be challenged by the observation that "God even loves Osama bin Laden."

Some will be deeply offended that Mother Crafton goes on to speak in such sympathetic detail about the destruction of the Palestinian homeland. That she does so in almost the same breath as her depiction of the settling of America as genocide will surely dislodge complacent hearts. Even closer to the bone, she will compel us to ask what justice was to be found in the handling of John Walker Lindh by our judicial system.

How can a book so offensive be so compactly and beautifully written?

The answer is in part that the author never scolds. The answer is also that beauty and truth are never too far apart. Crafton's rhythms of short and long sentences, the juxtaposition of particular and general observation, and the movement from quotation of colloquial Everyone to profound reflection, all embrace us in a way that makes it safe, safe at last, to look hard at 9/11. In and with the looking comes a sound as well: a word of grace that enables change. Good liturgy does it like that.

~ *Paul Marshall, Bishop of Bethlehem, Pennsylvania*

Introduction
Why a Mass?

I thought I would take the radio out into the garden so we could listen under the dogwood tree. So we sat, listening and drinking our tea. I wanted to hear the names of all the people I knew who had died, and I also wanted to hear the ethnic spread of all the names. Mayor Giuliani began it: *Aboud*, he read, several times. *Acevido. Ali.* The As lasted a long time. I didn't have anybody I knew until the Bs. *Andersen. Anderson. Atkins.*

Once in a while I got up to water a plant or prune something. I transplanted half a dozen tiny hollyhocks, in the hope that they will winter over successfully and come up in the spring. *DeArio. Dennaro. Dennison. Denton.*

We skipped an opportunity to add to our small but exquisite collection of American oratorical gems by recycling the Gettysburg Address instead. I'm assuming this was because Mario Cuomo is no longer governor, and so the planners quietly bowed to the current dearth of available public eloquence. President Lincoln stepped easily up to the plate, proving once again that, while there isn't much immortal about us, words come close.

And the names themselves were eloquence enough for the day.

The day was hard. It was hard to be alone and hard to be in company. You just didn't know where you wanted to be. It was hard to concentrate. It was hard not to worry about an anniversary attack.

Already word and image fatigue had set in as we approached the anniversary of the attacks on New York and the Pentagon, the horribly inconclusive Pearl Harbor of our uncertain days, inaugurating everything but a sure response. Were we at war? We were not sure, although the invasion of Iraq was just a few months in the future. If we were, then against whom? Where were the terrorists? Was Saddam going to stand in for them? Unable to find them, would we spend our fury on him instead, and tell ourselves that we had dealt with them in destroying him?

Meanwhile we used wistful words like "quiet" and "low-key" to describe the observances we planned for the day itself. A minute of silence sounded a lot better to many than an hour of speeches. Already people talked of just staying home, of not doing anything much. We knew they were still heartbroken, and that it made them tired. We preachers knew it because we were still heartbroken ourselves.

It was hard to find the right words to read for the evening service. I fussed with my talk, and timed it, threw things out and put them back in, much more preparation than I usually do for a three minute talk. I had no confidence in my words. I had no confidence in anything. I didn't want to go to the Cathedral; I wanted to stay home.

The train stations were full of soldiers and cops. They

were young. They were there to protect us. They were darling. I prayed that God would protect them.

People were already streaming into the Cathedral half an hour before the service began. Young people. Older people. Children. Everyone. About two thousand already, if I judged the seating capacity right, and more on the way. You looked west on 112th Street and saw them coming, filling the sidewalks, coming from the south along Amsterdam, from the North, alighting from city buses, getting out of yellow taxicabs. The love of God bathed them all in a holy light. Perhaps it was only the light of the dying day, but to me it seemed like the light of Christ.

The Cathedral grew dark and the service began. The music was the music of the world: an Iranian singer, a Jewish group, a DJ, Ritchie Havens stood alone on the stage and sang simply, that voice from our youth; still the Ritchie we remembered, only older and gray-bearded now, his beautiful hands moving in slow gestures that danced his words. The Bang on a Can Festival was there, or part of it, playing the new music with which they regularly supply hip New York in this sacred setting and feeling perfectly at home: strange, quiet music that floated up high in the Cathedral and then all around us.

We heard the music and the brief words in between the music, and our hearts began to heal a little. The music showed our healing: it became stronger, more joyful, its beat contagious as a smile. We began to clap, and the lead singer smiled and opened her arms to us, inviting more. Damaged and still bleeding, we nonetheless could not help but respond. After the service, my husband and I stood with the parents of a young man who had perished on that day. Same age as my husband's dead son. The two fathers shook each other's hands, looked into each other's eyes.

Out on the street afterwards, over to Broadway. Dinner with friends. "Hi, Mom," I heard, and turned around: there were Anna and Robert. She was just coming from an evening class at the Bank Street School. "I was hoping I might see you," I said, and they joined us for dinner. The restaurant was full. The streets were also full: full of students, old people, young people, people up to no good, children up past their bedtimes. The wind had died down, and the night was clear. It was still New York, and we were still here.

The Mass is celebrated by those of us who are still here.

As bruised as we are, we're still here. We're still bleeding, but our streets are not filled with dust today, nor with the smell of death. Not today. Not any more, and not yet. We're still alive. Still have the chance to savor being alive.

The Mass is celebrated by those of us who are still here.

In it we hear words of peace and reconciliation. We hear about how to handle offense, how to bring about forgiveness and reconciliation, how to handle the terrible anger of an unavenged wound. About how human aggression looks to God, and what God does about it. About the inclusive love of God, love that includes even people we might rather *not* include—there are times in human history when such decisions are best not left to us.

I want a kiss from your lips/ I want an eye for an eye, sings Bruce Springsteen, the bard of an American era toward the end of the century just past, an era we remember well. He has returned to help us speak. His songs have sometimes been uncritically adopted as jingoist anthems, but that works only if you don't go beyond the unforgettable refrains: *"Booo-orn in the USA"*. Bruce is a lot smarter than he seems. He sings of us, of how mixed we are, of how we can never have what we want, of how sometimes we shouldn't have it, of how we long for the past and can never return there.

Yes, we may want an eye for an eye. We may want vengeance, and we may want it bad. But vengeance is about the past, and human society can only stand if those who husband it keep their eyes steadfastly on the future. Live in the past and you are certain to die. Old wrongs cannot be redressed. What has been done cannot be undone. The dead cannot rise, not here. We can never make it right again, not as it was before. All we can do is protect the future, act in such a way that life together will somehow be possible again.

I hear the blood of my blood/ cryin' from the ground, Bruce sings. Yes. But the blood is life, the ancients believed, and life cries for life, not for death. Blood is not honored by more blood. Life is not honored by more death. Life is honored by more life, life well-lived, life lived on behalf of the dead from whom life was snatched too soon, life long and good, life laid gently down when it has finished its work and can sleep at last, satisfied.

If we respond to danger, let it be only to prevent more danger. If we move against an enemy, let it be only to prevent further evil. And let God have the vengeance, only God. It is not safe with us.

Let us go forth in the name of Christ.
The Geranium Farm
Autumn, 2002

1

Introit
New York, Autumn 2001

Nobody can concentrate on anything. The new attention span is something under five minutes, and then you're out of your chair or staring out the window or phoning somebody, those of us who still have phones that work. People are canceling things right and left: meetings, training sessions, even spiritual direction appointments—which may not be a very good idea.

I long to cancel things, too, but I don't. I *add* things. A prayer vigil at the church. Then one every night this week. People come to the simple services and stay after to sit in the candlelight and pray. A neighbor embraces me at the chapel door. "Thank you for being here," she whispers. I honestly don't know what "being there" accomplishes, but it seems to be all anybody can do. I don't think she means just me; she means St. Clement's. All the churches are doing pretty well at "being there" these days, and people are flocking to them. I look at her and see that her face looks pretty much like my face. We are showing our age this week: deep ruts under our eyes, no color in our cheeks.

But we cling together, friends and strangers. We sit and stand and kneel in song and in prayer. And in silence, long silence, silence that slows the breath and the pulse; that unclenches the hands and unhunches the shoulders. Silence that lets you hear your heartbeat again, lets you know that your blood still courses in its kindly stream through your body. Your blood is in your body. The Blood of Christ is in the chalice. His flesh reposes, a perfect china-white disk, on the paten. It is a perfect thin circle; almost thin enough to go under a microscope. If it were under a microscope, you would see that the circle is made of fine white flour and water. Physically, it isn't bone, and it isn't flesh. It's bread. Physically, there is only wine. There isn't any blood.

There isn't much blood at the place where the World Trade Center was either. It has all boiled away, or it has mixed with the white dust that coats everything, or it is buried under the rubble, motionless in the veins of those still to be discovered.

I see no reason to cancel the Spanish Mass at St. Clement's. Maria and her mother attend, as they do most Tuesday nights. The little congregation is mostly children and their mothers and teachers, and we always eat supper together after Mass.

Maria is thirteen years old. She is beautiful, with a silky fall of black hair almost to her waist and large dark eyes, like the eyes of a fawn. She helps the younger children in the after-school program with their homework and with their drawings. They all want to draw the World Trade Center. Their drawings are all similar: the two towers, smoking like chimneys. Most of the towers have windows like the frame windows in a house. In some of the windows the children have drawn people frowning and crying, "Help!" in those speech balloons you see in cartoons. In a couple of the drawings, unhappy people hurtle to the ground, their mouths all upside down "U"s in the limited lexicon of elementary school art. Firemen and their trucks cluster at the foot of the towers or scale the sides. One of the firemen is saying, "I'll save you." He is smiling, his mouth a self-confident "U."

Maria helps the little ones draw, but she does not draw herself. She is growing up now. I have known her since she was six and first started coming to St. Clement's after school. We have talks that are getting to be like grownup talks. She is right on the cusp, between child and woman, inhabiting that brief moment when you can go back and forth between the two, before you are trapped in adulthood forever.

Now she leans forward, ignoring her plate of food. She has something important to say. "You know what I'm afraid of?"

"What's that?"

"What if the rescue workers give up too soon and the bulldozers come and bury the people who are in the basement?" she says. "Because I think they're still alive down there."

"You do?"

Maria nods vigorously. "Yes. I *know* they are. You know those restaurants and the little shops down there? Well, the people could live a long time down there, because there's food in the restaurants and food and candy in the little stores, and there are bottles of water and juice. They have tons of water there. So I'm afraid the rescue workers'll give up and those people will be buried alive."

I touch her mother's arm under the table and we exchange a slight, sad glance. Who's going to tell her that the restaurants in the lower level of the World Trade Center are packed tightly with the compacted remains of the first fifteen floors of the building and everything and everybody that was in them. That the refrigerated cases of water and juice and cartons of milk are now as flat as a greeting card, buried under countless tons of masonry and steel and human flesh, that nobody is left to sit at the tables and wait for rescue. We say nothing, and I stroke Maria's beautiful hair. My touch changes something: I watch her cross over, right there in front of us, a silent young woman where a moment ago sat a hopeful child. *Go back and forth as long as you can, my little friend. Stay in the shelter of your own hope for as long as you can. There will come a time when you can no longer find your way there.*

Actually, I'm sure Maria knew they were dead already. I knew it as she spoke. And *she* knows that *I* know—there is a flicker of knowing in her eyes. The dream of the people in the restaurants, waiting patiently for help to arrive, was a story she invited us to share, a story she could enter but into which we could not follow. Not any more.

But in the Mass, we enter it. We enter this story and many like it. The saints and angels join us in the Mass, we are told. We say so every time we celebrate it: *Therefore we praise you, joining our voices with angels and archangels and with all the company of heaven.* The ancients believed that the dead participated with the church from their place in the kingdom of heaven. Dead to this world, they live in Christ and feast forever, we say, at the heavenly banquet of which our chaste bit of bread and sip of wine is a foretaste.

The dead do not wait for us at the bottom of the World Trade Center. They make no use of what is there, for there is nothing of any use there. But Maria's childish story invites me to enter the true story in which I place my hope. They may not feast here, but they feast there.

"Look at this," Bobby says. We're in the parish office; Bobby's opening the mail. He holds up a photocopied drawing. It shows the two towers exploding, and upon the cloud of smoke and debris that billows from them rise scores of little figures. They are the dead. Jesus towers over them, his arms spread in welcome, gathering them all up. At the bottom of the page it says that this drawing is the work of an eighth grade girl in another state.

Bobby has tears in his eyes. Bobby has a wisecracking outside and a soft inside. But I have tears in my eyes, too, as sentimental and childish as the drawing is. "We are both way too tired," I tell him, and he nods his head and smiles. But what the childish drawing shows really is what we believe to be true: straight to heaven they went, whatever heaven is. From the moment of death the larger life opened to them, and they stepped out into it. It is a life of which we are already a part but which we can barely imagine. And it is good, good beyond anything we know or can imagine.

Outside of St. Clement's, a shrine has grown up. There are shrines all over the city—the enormous one at Union Square, as close as most people can get to the site of the bombing. Shrines at most churches and at all the firehouses and police stations. The banks of photographs of the missing in the train stations and the Port Authority are becoming shrines, too, as the hope that put them there begins to fade. St. Clement's shrine is little: just a plain wooden cross against a red, white, and blue backing. Just a place for the neighbors to put candles. One of the flight attendants lived a couple of doors down from the church. A young woman across the street lost her firefighter fiancé, and our two nearest fire stations each lost more than half their people.

Bobby put the shrine together. He hasn't slept for days, not since the bombing, I think. I keep seeing little things he has done: I notice that our fax cover sheets now have "The Light is On. God Bless America" emblazoned across the bottom. He attempts to do the same with our letterhead, but I dissuade him. In the paper, one of our large churches is pictured raising the American flag in its sanctuary while the congregation sings "God Bless America."

Instead, at St. Clement's, Matt orders a thousand large blue lapel buttons that say "Peace" in Arabic and in English. *Salaam.* We pass them out to everyone we see, especially to the owners of the *bodegas* in our neighborhood, most of whom are related and from Yemen. We make them available to the diocese, and people order them from us. We wear them everywhere. Some people ask us where they can get one and we take ours off and hand it over. Other people are angry when they see that the Arabic script. Somehow the buttons balance out all the flags a little. If God blessing America means that the love of God flows towards us more than it does towards our enemies, how universal a god do we have? God loves the people of Afghanistan, too, and the people of Iraq. God even loves Osama bin Laden, gripped as he is by evil. We are not the only ones whose hearts are broken by what has happened. God's heart is broken, too.

And so is my heart. I show it in odd ways. Can't sleep, of course, and cry several times a day, of course. But I also have lost, quite abruptly, a one-a-day and sometimes two-a-day murder mystery habit that goes back years. Lost it without even thinking about it. Just noticed, sometime in mid-October, that I hadn't read a murder mystery in weeks, hadn't finished the one I had been reading on the train the morning of September 11, and wasn't remotely curious about how it ended. That I had no desire to read another one. I had always found them relaxing, those page turners, relaxing in direct and strange proportion to their goriness and perversity, as if fictional evil were somehow talismanic against the encroachment of real evil into the world. But no more. I don't want to read about people deliberately hurting and killing other people any more. That I used to like these things seems to me now to be monstrous. The Hell humanity really creates is more than enough Hell for anyone.

People say the World Trade Center site is Hell, but I don't think so. It is a grave, and so it is holy, the spot in which souls have left their earthly homes for their heavenly one. Early in the days after the bombing, the mountain of rubble is so huge that I know it will never be cleaned up. Never. And each time I go, I am amazed at how much the workers *have* cleaned up, but still more amazed at how much is left. This will never be finished, I think.

I am standing at the place where the concourse, through which I passed every day for years, used to be. It is below my feet, and I am on the pile above it, standing among twisted chunks of unidentifiable stuff, talking to two policemen. The bookstore in which I would stop now and then for a guilty pleasure is flat under my feet, all the books and all the sales clerks and the shoppers. So are the drug store and the cool little Coach store with all its handbags and the flower cart over near the escalators and all the flowers and the bank of ATM machines right across from them and all the money. I close my eyes and see the flattened escalators struggling to rise, the abandoned flattened telephones trying to ring, their smothered dial tones trying to sound, the twisted steel beams straining to straighten and stand, groaning like Samson and then failing under the weight, collapsing again with a final shudder and lying still. *It's no use*, they think in their inorganic version of despair. *No use.*

Windows on the World was lovely. Remember? I knew the sister of the pastry chef there. You sat and ate your meal, looking out at the whole island of Manhattan and the harbor and Staten Island and New Jersey out in the distance. On a foggy day, you were in the clouds. The restaurant gleamed with sleek brass railings and rich paneling, lit from an unseen source to a soft glow. When you came off the elevator, there was a huge crystal on a pedestal at the entrance, also lit so that it seemed to glow from within. Or was it a crystal? Now I'm not so sure. *Somebody*: what was at the entrance to Windows on the World? Wasn't it a huge crystal? Or have I already begun to forget?

There was a Miro in the lobby downstairs. The World Trade Center housed a wonderful art collection. It *was* a Miro, wasn't it?

The crystal exploded into a million pieces. Maybe it was a billion. Some of them were embedded in the steel beams.

Some of them were embedded in the flesh of people who shot through the air and through walls and windows and down, down. I think some of the pieces may be in my lungs, because some days when I was on the pile I didn't wear my respirator and now my chest hurts. Some of the pieces are on the ground, mixed with the white dust, the dust of cement and bone. I dig at the dust with the toe of my boot. I don't see any crystal sparkles.

The Miro crumpled along with the wall on which it hung. Now I guess it is down in the basement near where the PATH train was, all in pieces too small to identify. I guess Miro touched each piece of that painting with his own hands. Miro has been gone for a long time. Now his painting is gone, too. I think it was a Miro.

Now I see why the very first parts of the Gospel to be told and then written down were the passion narratives. I never really understood that before. People wanted to tell the story before they forgot. It was so terrible, they had to tell each other and tell each other. Everyone says something different, something especially his. Or hers. There were dozens of gospels, we know, before Matthew, Mark, Luke and John emerged victorious as canon. Of course there were. This story bore telling and re-telling, again and again. Everyone wanted to tell.

We know that the resurrection stories came later, added to the passion narratives, perhaps by other hands. This, too, makes sense: the event of resurrection is full of mystery and misunderstanding. We can't encompass a thing like that in the world of our experience. But we do know death. We can talk about death. We can write about death, because we have seen death. We hang back before the risen Christ because we do not understand him. And because our sorrow blinds us—the dust of it gets in our eyes and in our mouths and throats and all over us, so that we even smell like it. Our protective gear doesn't really protect us. "We are unprotected and unprotectable," a man told me the other day, and he was right.

And so we linger over the eighth-grader's drawing of Jesus sweeping up the dead in his arms of love, thousands of them all at once, longing for it to be true.

I think it is true. I know it is. I know it.

2

Kyrie Eleison
But why Do They Hate us?

People refused to fly on airplanes because other people who looked Middle Eastern were on board. A Sikh was beaten by a crowd because of his turban. Another Sikh wrote in to *The Times* to explain what a Sikh was. An Indian gas station owner was murdered out West somewhere because somebody couldn't tell he was Indian. Some American Muslim women left off covering their heads, out of fear. Others took it up, out of solidarity. My friend Tom, a professor of comparative religion and an Islamicist, preached and taught everywhere about what *jihad* really means. It refers to an inner struggle, usually, unless one is faced with a force attempting to prevent Muslim observance—as nobody in the World Trade Center or the Pentagon seems to have been doing that morning in September. "How's it going?" I asked him recently. "You wouldn't believe how much work I'm getting out of this," he said, ruefully. "Everybody wants me to come and tell them what *jihad* is."

Late at night, I ran into Helen and Richie on the train coming home. They had worked all day at St. Paul's

Chapel, serving coffee and fluffing pillows and giving out eye drops and sandwiches to workers at the WTC site. They were exhausted but exhilarated. Working at St. Paul's was like that. Strange: you're in a place surrounded on all sides by tragedy, but being there makes you feel something like joy. Or maybe this is not so strange.

The train clanked along through the night. It was crowded. Richie found a seat a few rows back and sat quietly. His wife and I sat together. She talked in the manner of one who has been through something too important to set aside quickly: how grateful the firefighters and cops and rescue workers were, what an honor it was to serve them. We talked on, now about the war itself, what seemed to be happening over there, what might be ahead. Then Helen had a question.

"You know, maybe *you* understand," she said. "I really don't understand why all this has happened. I mean, I know the bombers were sick people, but what about the people who were glad it happened? On television, you know, when they showed them dancing and laughing about it? What did we do that made them want to kill so many of us? Why do they hate us?"

I have wanted to preach about this, but so far I haven't. People have been too fragile, and too angry. Truth to tell, I've been too ragged myself and, to tell a further truth, too angry. A skateboarder cruised past me on Eighth Avenue on my way to the church one day, chanting "Arabics Go Home." *Since when is "Arabic" a noun, moron?* I had asked him silently, one of the many silences enjoined upon clergy, silences sometimes difficult to maintain: You can't call somebody "moron" out on the street on Sunday morning when you're in clerical attire. I came into the church mad, heart-pounding mad. Everywhere, racism was donning the clothes of patriotism, and we were all supposed to applaud. I felt a crusading desire to rebuke it. I have learned to be careful of myself when I want to crusade. I am apt to let my righteous indignation get so far away from me that it ceases to be very righteous at all. I knew that my hearers needed comfort from me more than they needed prophecy. That there would be time for prophecy, time and necessity, but that what we all needed right now was first aid.

But now Helen was *asking*. Maybe it was time for my sermon, a sermon spoken, not preached, to a quiet, gentle woman who simply wanted to know: *Why do they hate us?*

Those who claim responsibility for terrorist actions in the Middle East almost always reference the state of Israel and the Palestinians. Terrorists from other Middle Eastern countries do this, even in situations that seemingly have nothing to do with Israel or the Palestinians. This strikes many Americans as odd, even false: "Sure, people have political opinions, but why would you kill somebody over what's happening in somebody else's country?" they wonder. "I mean, my dad's Irish, and I think the Brits ought to get out of there, but you don't see me blowing things up."

People suspect that the Israeli-Palestinian situation is just an excuse, that terrorists don't really care about it at all and that their real goal is just to kill people. And indeed, the real goal of a terrorist *is* to kill. They *are* sick. Their action is evil. But it's not true that the issue they're ready to kill for is not a real issue for them. Or, for that matter, for us, if we ever want to get out of the current situation with some of us still alive.

If we cannot find a way to separate our war against terror from our capacity for self-criticism, we're in for more trouble where this trouble came from. While it is not true that we "had this coming"—nothing could justify the attacks on 9/11/01—we must nonetheless examine ourselves so that we can understand who we are and who we have been in the world. We did *not* have this coming, but to the extent that we have played a role in our own sorrows at all, it would be a good idea for us to change what we can and become better than we are. We should always want to become better than we are. Everybody should want that.

We must begin with a willingness to question any self-analysis in which we look too good. Every moral agent must do this. The suggestion that we engage in self-examination should not be viewed by anyone as unpatriotic or treasonous. Nobody—no individual and no nation—is always righteous. We are all profoundly mixed.

So where does the terrible anger against us in the Arab world come from? What, if anything, does our behavior in the world have to do with it? Why is Israel consistently the focus of that anger? Most Americans honestly don't know. Most Americans—even those who were alive at the time—either do not know or have forgotten the circumstances surrounding the creation of the state of Israel.

After the second World War, the allies knew that large numbers of European Jews would have to be resettled somewhere. But where? Where else but in Palestine, the land from which they had dispersed almost two thousand years before? It was their promised land from ancient times. Their scriptures and the Christian ones spoke of it thus innumerable times. As the terrible details of the

Holocaust filtered out of Germany and Eastern Europe and into the newsreels, decent people everywhere knew that simple justice required assistance from the world community in building new lives out of broken ones in whatever way possible.

Of course Palestine was where they should go.

Palestine was what it was called until 1948. Not *Israel.* Look at a map from that era.

Conveniently, the British *ran* Palestine. It had been a protectorate since 1918. Look to this time, the time after World War I, not to the Six Day Way or to 1948, to understand.

Great Britain was the mandated power for Palestine after the victors in the first World War divided the spoils in the Middle East. But the Palestinians had lived in this land ever since the Jews dispersed from it in the first century. Some Jews, of course, never left, and they and their Arab neighbors had continued to live there. Centuries passed. A couple of crusades brought European armies to the Holy Land, militant in the conviction that the people there were heathens and had no right to be there beyond what Europeans might choose to allow. And a growing exodus of European Jews to Palestine had been underway since the latter years of the nineteenth century, swelling to large numbers in the 1930s as the threat of Nazism loomed over Eastern Europe and then swallowed it whole.

Jewish emigration to Palestine had been encouraged by Zionist leaders in Great Britain since the nineteenth century. They hoped that the population of Palestine would undergo a demographic shift, with larger and larger waves of Jewish immigration eventually resulting in a Jewish majority. The British government supported this dream:

His Majesty's Government views with favour
the establishment in Palestine of a national
home for the Jewish people, and will use their
best endeavours to facilitate the achievement of
this object, it being clearly understood that
nothing shall be done which may prejudice the
civil and religious rights of existing non-Jewish
communities in Palestine or the rights and political status enjoyed by Jews in any other country.

~ *The Balfour Declaration*, 1917

The Palestinian people had not been not consulted
about the creation of Israel as a Jewish State, a process
which was already well underway by the time the second
World War ended. No Palestinians were among its architects, even though they lived there: over a million of them
at the time, as against 50,000 Jews. The policies toward
Jewish immigration to Palestine were policies of the Great
Powers, arising from their needs. The decisions that would
eventually bring about the state of Israel were made by the
British, the French and, of course, the Americans. "A land
without people for a people without a land," was how
enthusiasts envisioned it. I don't know what term they used
for the beings who lived in Palestine at the time, but I guess
they weren't *people*.

Of course the Jews would go there after the horrors of
the Holocaust. There were no people there.

Does any of this may have a familiar ring? It should, to
Americans. It should remind us of ourselves. We know that
treaties with Native American tribes were occasionally
signed, first by the English and then by the American fed-

eral government, but the treaties that mattered were the ones between Europeans. And we know that treaties with Native Americans were routinely broken if circumstances demanded it. We remember learning in school that white Americans in the nineteenth century considered it their God-given right to own the land, and we remember from our school days what this was called: "Manifest Destiny." Domination of the continent on which we lived was not just our desire; it was God's. The goal of Manifest Destiny—"to over spread and to possess the whole of the continent which Providence has given us"[1]—drove our westward expansion across the plains, over the Rockies and all the way to the rocky Pacific coast. It seemed obvious, a clear indication of God's will. *Manifest.*

This destiny was by no means as manifest to Native Americans as it was to European Americans. When they retaliated, we found it savage. Sometimes it was. They tried desperately to resist us. With our superior firepower, we almost eradicated them as a race.

We have come late to the recognition of this national sin. No American over fifty learned in school about the expansion of the American West in terms of genocide. We received it as Anglo heroism versus Indian savagery. Now we mythologize the Indians and revere their ways, admire their spirituality; sometimes even attempt to appropriate it. We almost wiped them out. Now we spend thousands of dollars on one of their gorgeous handmade pots.

---

1 Newspaper editor John L. O'Sullivan originated this famous phrase in 1845. A Northerner, his reputation was permanently tarnished by his support of slavery just prior to the Civil War.

A new nation, fired by a spiritual experience of its own chosen-ness, convinced that God has given over a land occupied by others into its hands. *Israel. Frontier America. Manifest Destiny. Providence. Zionism.* Quite apart from issues of access to oil and to a Persian Gulf waterway, quite apart from our need for a strategic location for a military presence in the Middle East, quite apart from the politics of the years following the first World War, we identify spiritually with the experience of the state of Israel because it reminds us of our powerful mythology about ourselves. We have confused Israeli settlers with our own frontiersmen.

Or maybe that is not what we have done. Maybe we have understood them both correctly. Maybe they are exactly the same. Maybe the drive for expansion is so familiar to us that we cannot see, as we could not see in the nineteenth century, that the idea of Manifest Destiny leads inevitably to genocide.

A destiny manifest to those who claim it. Not so clear to those who must surrender to it.

Outside observers of our behavior—and some critics within, even in the nineteenth century, like some critics within Judaism who questioned the Zionist project from its inception—long ago concluded that we do not understand indigenous peoples to *have* rights in land or the fruits of land we want for ourselves. We may say we do, and we may believe ourselves when we say it. But sometimes we behave otherwise. Strange as it ought to seem, for a nation that began its life in a storied revolt from a colonial overlord, we behave like a colonial power ourselves. Still. We do not own colonies, but we continue to view third-world nations—some of them former protectorates and current territories—as *instrumentally* important, not intrinsically so. We cannot seem to help believing that they continue to exist for our benefit. We have become accustomed to it, and our prosperity demands it. It is what we are used to. We are perfectly willing to grant them land we don't want. We want them to have work and productivity, but not at the cost of disturbing the weighting of the world's wealth in our corner. We are willing to honor the peculiar beauties of their cultures, but only as archeological or anthropological curiosities. And not at all if it stands in the way of our getting something we want.

That part of the human family that refers to itself as the *first world* has yet to shed the burden of having owned other people and countries. We point to our foreign aid, our development advice, our technological assistance, our many national kindnesses as reasons to overlook that aspect of our history, but it remains. "You used to control us," they think when they look at us, "and sometimes you still do."

We want the oil that flows sluggishly beneath the sandy plains of the Middle East. We have little interest in changing—even slightly—the bloated lifestyle we refer to as "The American Dream." Our houses, our automobiles— like our stomachs—grow larger every year. Our passionate defense of Israel's right to exist would be a very different thing if there were no oil in the Persian Gulf, if there were no Suez Canal through which oil could be shipped. Allied with the British Government, whose leaders were the architects of the creation of a Jewish State in Palestine, we needed a client state in that part of the world, and we need one still. Here is how the British looked at the area in 1915.

The British annexation of Palestine [where] we
might plant three or four million European
Jews...should Palestine fall within the British
sphere of influence, and should Britain encourage a Jewish settlement there, as a British
dependency, we could have in twenty to thirty
years a million Jews out there—perhaps more;
they would...form a very effective guard for the
Suez Canal...England...would have in the
Jews the best possible friends, who would be the
best national interpreters of ideas in the eastern
countries and would serve as a bridge between
the two civilizations. That again is not a mate-
rial argument, but certainly it ought to carry
great weight with any politician who likes to
look fifty years ahead." [2]

So what's wrong with that? What is so sinister about this
note from one governmental official to another, at the
beginning of the last century? There was nothing wrong
with finding a homeland for the Jews. There was nothing
wrong with honoring their desire for restoration to the
Promised Land of their communal memory.

These are not terrible things. But the casual assumption
that the fates of other nations and peoples can and should
be manipulated to suit the interests of powerful nations is
chilling. It has lasted into the present, and it has colored it

---

2 Memorandum, "The Future of Palestine," Herbert Samuel to Prime
Minister Asquith. Samuel would later become the first High
Commissioner of Palestine under the British Mandate.

profoundly. The savvy politicians of 1915, looking fifty years ahead into a confident future, would have done well to ask themselves what things might have looked like in a hundred years.

So it isn't just because the Jews suffered horribly during the war that we have supported them in Israel, although they did suffer horribly, and Allied advocacy of Zionism was certainly motivated in part by that horror. But we don't always assist those who suffer horribly. Not every time. When Turkey marched millions of Armenians far from their homes and massacred them, we did nothing: Turkey was an important ally in the Near East. When European Jews themselves had appealed for asylum before our entry into the second World War, we had turned some of them away. Our perceived self-interest lay elsewhere. When Iraq gassed thousands of Kurds into agonizing death or permanent disability, we did nothing. There was no oil under their control. When Ruwandan ethnic factions squared off against one another, slaughtering upwards of a million people before they were finished, we did not intervene. No oil under them, either.

And it isn't just because Saddam Hussein was a terrible dictator that we marched into Baghdad to unseat him. He was a terrible dictator twenty years ago, when we were supplying him with arms and money. We've done the same for many like him.

This is hard for us to hear. We're accustomed to thinking of ourselves as good, and as altruistically so. We always help defeat the oppressor. We always give. But the truth is, we *often* help and give. Often, but not always. We often help to defeat the oppressor—but there have been times when it has served our interests better to keep one in power, and we have done so without a qualm. We're proud of our revolutionary past—and justly so. But because you were morally courageous in one era doesn't mean that everything you do in another is wonderful, too, just because it's you doing it. Nobody owns the moral high ground, and nobody inherits it. Each generation must find it for itself.

So we can't see that we have become more like the power against which our forebears rebelled than like those plucky colonists of the eighteenth century, whose memory we so revere. We're not them any more. Haven't been for a long time. We're the overlords now.

American aid is often first on the ground where there is a disaster, and it is generous. We are justifiably proud of that. We are justly proud of the role we played in winning the second World War, too. We forget that Europeans have a slightly different memory of those days from the memories we have: we allowed Europe to suffer for two years before we joined them, and we might well have remained aloof from the European war altogether had not Pearl Harbor intervened.

Our pride in our better actions is simple, true, and well-founded. But the fact that we frequently exercise our great power in magnanimity doesn't mean that every way in which we exercise it is magnanimous.

Be careful how you bring this up in conversation. Especially now. It won't go well.

Our inability to question ourselves with seriousness leads us into absurd situations. Our leaders often lecture other nations about their human rights violations, as if we didn't have any. Meanwhile, it seems not to register with us that the only other countries that have the death penalty are the countries we lecture: China, Saudi Arabia (we don't lecture the Saudis too much, counting on their support in the Middle East), Iraq, Iran, Libya—not the company we like to imagine ourselves keeping.

Be careful with this one, too. Maybe you shouldn't bring it up: it's not worth it.

"They just don't like us because we're free," is what we usually tell ourselves. "That's what it is." We honestly can't think of anything we've done to them. We know that colonialism had to end, but we don't know—refuse to know—how long its fallout has lasted, and how intimately we were involved in it. But we were in it up to our necks, and it lasts a long time. "That stuff happened a long time ago," we say. Yes, it did, but we still benefit from it every day.

Because it has left us very rich. We consume many times the resources consumed by the people of poor countries, and we have no interest in changing that. If they were richer, their goods would cost us more, and we might not have as many of them. Our "footprint" is large, our impact on the environment much larger than those of people in India, or Indonesia, or Malaysia, or Africa, or anywhere else. We have twenty pairs of shoes each. They have one. Or none. We have our own bedrooms, several cars, family rooms, three or four televisions. We use hundreds of gallons of water, hundreds of liters of oil, hundreds of acres of grain for every one of these used by these people so far away from us in miles and in experience. We take up more room. And we refuse to take up less.

This is ridiculous, traitorous nonsense. Those Palestinian kids dancing in the streets after 9/11 never even heard of Manifest

Destiny. They don't know what the Balfour Declaration was. Those things have nothing to do with terrorism. That's a smoke screen for their own hate.

No. You don't have to understand a complex problem to participate violently in it. Not understanding, in fact, is what facilitates your violence. It is those who fail to understand who rush to arms, not those who understand.

Did the young people we watched dancing in the streets of Gaza after the September 11th bombing know about the American doctrine of Manifest Destiny? Had they studied the history of Zionism in England in the early years of the twentieth century, considered the curious collision between the democratic ideals of the early twentieth century and the lingering baggage the Great Powers carried as colonial occupiers, ultimately unwilling to divest themselves of their holdings? Had those young people studied the League of Nations, with its lofty commitment to national sovereignty and self-determination, and understood that it actually failed because the Great Powers would have had to give up too much of the power they wielded over what would come to be known as the *third world*, and that the most vigorous objections to it originated within the Congress of the United States

No. They don't know any of these things. But they do know about our footprint. They know that we are rich and they know that they are poor, and they know we support and protect the government that restricts their travel and bulldozes their houses, in whose country they have lived their whole lives in squalid camps, the government that displaced their grandparents from houses whose addresses they still remember as home, even though they have never lived in or even seen those houses. Their homes become more beautiful in their imaginations every day, lovelier than they could ever have been in real life. Gardens grow around them, date and fig trees burst into mythic bloom they never knew sixty years ago, long before these children dancing in the street were born. "Right of Return" is what it's called: the right to live in those magical houses of memory again someday—a phrase used first by returning Jews to describe and explain *their* re-entry into the land their forebears had left centuries before. A day that will never come for the Palestinians, no matter how long their forebears lived there, no matter what happens.

So what *does* happen when a person grows up knowing that his situation can never change? When he grows up knowing that it won't matter what he does, for he will never be freer and more prosperous than someone else's interests grant him to be? That he is not a person of worth, that his claim to an ancient home is a lesser claim than someone else's ancient claim? And that this is all somehow related to his religion and to theirs, to something called the Crusades, to a pair of wars in which he and his people did not fight and in whose terms of surrender they did not participate? That there is not and never can be a legitimate way to change his lot?

He will find an illegitimate way.

Terrorism is illegitimate. It defines illegitimacy. But it does not arise in a vacuum.

Over the long span of the history of the two faiths, it really has not been the case that Muslims hated Jews. Together, Muslims and Jews formed the cadre of scholars and artists who preserved most of what we have inherited from the ancient world, perilously close to being lost in what is remembered in Northern Europe as the Dark Ages. Jewish statesmen and scholars held influential positions in the Moorish kingdoms of Spain for most of the seven centuries of Muslim presence in Spain. After this rich epoch of creative coexistence ended, when Christianity reasserted its exclusive claims and retooled mosques into churches, when the Inquisition began to persecute many of its own, along with anybody else who looked suspicious— Jews who escaped its dangers often fled to Muslim countries. They knew they would be safe there, and they were, finding refuge in the ancient Near Eastern tradition of hospitality to the stranger.

Muslim anti-Semitism is relatively new. Christian anti-Semitism is much older. Which is one of the things that makes our current situation very odd indeed. Christian fundamentalists, who make headlines now and then declaring confidently that God does not hear the prayers of Jews, and who pray earnestly for their conversion, now find themselves even more repulsed by Muslims, and make sudden, strange bedfellows with all manner of Zionist causes. The enemy of my enemy is my friend, I guess. Just today, a Christian movement in North Carolina to prohibit the inclusion of the Koran in a freshman world history survey course made the news. *Good Lord.* I wonder if we shouldn't stop using Arabic numerals, just to be on the safe side.

Since the attacks of September 11, 2001, many of us have become unable to hear criticism of our government and its actions. We have become even less able to do so since the invasion of Iraq. We have demonized our enemies. We have suggested that people who don't agree with our posture in the Middle East should be jailed or even killed without a fair trial. Too many religious people have jumped on the bandwagon of xenophobia out of love and fear for our sons and daughters overseas, out of intense grief for our beloved dead, and have understood our love and fear and grief to preclude independent thought and criticism of our government's policies.

But we're the ones with freedom of expression. America is all about criticism of our government, which we don't forbid and never have.

The Taliban did. The Taliban was like that. Saddam Hussein was like that. But we're not supposed to be. It's a weak person who can't bear to examine himself. And a weaker country than I ever thought we were.

And I thought we said they hate us because we're free.

3

Gloria
Peace where peace is to be found

The angels were the first to sing the *Gloria*, the first verse of it, anyway. The rest was added later on, to give it more heft. Then, for a long time, it was only sung when the bishop was in church—that was when they sang better than a lot of them do today, I guess. Then after a while we were allowed to sing it when only the priest and the people were there, but only on very special occasions: Easter and the anniversaries of the priests' own ordinations. Finally we could sing it every week, but it was moved to the end of the service. I always liked the *Gloria* at the end when I was little—because of the angels, of course, but also as a heartfelt hymn of thanksgiving that the service was finally over.

In penitential seasons we don't sing it at all, we sing a *Kyrie* instead: Lord, have mercy upon us. Or a threefold *Trisagion*. Holy God, Holy and Mighty, Holy immortal One, have mercy upon us. The reason we don't sing the *Gloria* in penitential seasons is because it's not fitting. High rejoicing doesn't go with repentance and self-examination—which is why it hasn't been the easiest thing in the world to write one for this book. I've put it off for as long as I could, but the publisher e-mailed me this evening, wondering where the manuscript might be.

It's all done except for the *Gloria*.

Maybe if I send it in with just the *Kyrie* he won't notice.

But he's a monk. He'll notice.

But how do you write a *Gloria* for a Mass in Time of War? There's no glory in a war. In what might we rejoice now, when we have lost so much and fear losing so much more? A *Gloria*? It isn't fitting.

A short one, then. One sung by the people, and not just when the clergy are around. A *Gloria* that will announce good tidings. But they will have to be tidings we can believe.

Glory to God in the highest, and peace to God's people on earth. That there would be glory to God and peace on earth sung in one breath, that the angels would see one as a corollary of the other. That God's glory is tied up with human peace. That peace is about life here on earth as well as about the hope of heaven—that these things are assumed gives me hope: at least the people who wrote the Bible are thinking of peace.

But it's been so long since then.

When the angels sang of peace over the same terrain that is now so drenched with human blood, there wasn't peace on earth. Israel was under the heel of an occupying government. Life was violent then, too. And their song didn't inaugurate peace on earth either. They sang it and flew away, and the fields over which they had hovered were unchanged. The shepherds were still shepherds, and still poor. The Romans were still in charge. It still wasn't fair. Nothing had changed.

And then here *we* came with the angels' song: the church. Bishops in the finest clothes we could find for them, finer and finer all the time, singing the hymn angels had sung to the ragged child born in a stable. We gave admiring lip service to his poverty, his homelessness, his powerlessness, but we couldn't help arranging ourselves as if the poverty in which Jesus chose to be born and live were and aberration. We built our churches, as soon as it was safe to build them at all, in the same architectural style as the imperial power built its halls of judgment. We enthroned the clergy in it, and we have struggled with their enthronement ever since. We all but crown our bishops, and then we're angry with them when they act like kings. We show forth the power of power to corrupt us at the same time as we warn against it.

No wonder people have a hard time with us. We have a hard time with ourselves.

Islam exalted the power of God, but understood the power of all human beings before God to be equal. In that, it radically democratized human faith; as in Buddhism, in Islam the wealthiest person was on no firmer a footing than the poorest. Each had a direct line of prayer to God. There was no Church to mediate this access. There were no priests. The imam was a scholar, but anyone could follow the path.

Maybe this doesn't sound much like the Taliban to you. But then, the Army of God, with its weird theology that finds it possible to embrace murder as a means of preventing the death of the unborn, doesn't sound much like us. Things get out of hand in religious circles pretty easily.

The first New Testament angel breaks the news to Mary

about her unusual pregnancy. The next ones sing the song of peace. The ones after that feed a starving Jesus in the wilderness. The next ones guard the empty tomb. The angels after that get the apostles out of jail.

And the next ones are very different. They appear in the book of Revelation, the last book in the canon. They appear in an expectation of the future, and they are at the head of an army. As if the work of the other angels, the peace ones, the ones who get you out of jail and open the tomb, had not intervened. The militaristic angels of Revelation are unrelated to the story of Jesus: they are soldiers. They sound more like they belong in our story.

What would it take for the song of the angels to come true? What would it take for God to be glorified by peace on earth? Maybe it depends on whose story we're telling. Are we telling the old story of human hatred and lust for power? The story we know best? Or can we tell a new one?

Is it reasonable to hope for a world without war? Not if we're telling the old story.

Glory to God in the highest, and peace to God's people on earth.

Or maybe we don't know what glory is. The human glory I have seen has always stood right next to injustice and suffering. I might not have recognized it if it had stood anywhere else.

Late on a weeknight in New York, the theatre lights at St. Clement's were still on. People streamed in the doors, coming from other theaters. Performers rushed in from their shows, still in their makeup—big names, some of them, the kind of people who travel with bodyguards. It was the tenth anniversary of the Tiananmen Square uprising, and the actors read letters and memoirs from survivors and relatives of victims of that terrible time.

These were great actors: Corin Redgrave, Kevin Spacey, Brian Dennehey, Kathleen Chalfant. Two, three hours went by, and they continued to read as people sat in the seats and on the steps and stood in the dark to listen. They became the dead—young people from the other side of the world, people they would never meet, people nobody will ever meet again because they were struck down in the springtime of their youth. And we became families of the dead, became their mothers and fathers, their sisters and brothers, their friends, those who mourned them, those who were fired by their courage to look toward a better day. We left the church full of the power of words and the grace given the actor to bring them to life.

The organizers of the evening were Chinese dissidents who now live outside of China. Some were relatives of people who had died. Some had witnessed the massacre. They spoke with quiet determination of a time when things would not be as they are there. Although they had seen inhumanity, they chose to hope for something different.

That was glory: a song about peace before there is any peace to be seen.

Years ago, while I served on the waterfront of New York, I approached a ship for a routine visit. But something was not right: what looked to be most of the crew was up on the deck at the top of the gangway, and a policeman stood uneasily at the bottom, not sure of what to do. It was revealed that the owner was in financial trouble and had stopped paying the crew several months back, an old maritime story. They were Pakistani, all of them except for one or two Bangladeshi and an Egyptian steward. They were refusing to work the ship until they were paid, and the captain had just attempted to assault an officer with a steel bar. Then he had summoned the police to arrest the crew and take them off the ship, to jail, and then to deportation with a black mark on their passports.

How would they prevail? They were weak and few in number. They did not vote here, nor did the laws of their country apply here. They were at the mercy of the company, and they knew no one here who could help them.

But with considerable courage and some good advice, they helped themselves. They threw a bed sheet with STRIKE painted on it in red over the gangway railing. Now this was a job action. *Oh.* The police understood that; they were union themselves. They knew what a strike was. They knew that their duty was to protect the strikers and the company alike. Nobody was throwing anybody out of anything until it was settled, and nobody was going to get hurt.

It was glorious. People from so far away, protected by a common understanding of the power of collective action among workers. People who didn't want to do right by their employees, forced to do so. People who, in their own country, had reason to fear the police—protected by the police in our country. People who summoned the courage not to give up and give in, eventually winning their point and returning home with their wages in their pockets. Dignity and honor. Won without bloodshed.

I took the crew out to dinner the night they were to leave for home. "This is the best night of my life," the chief engineer said, raising his glass in a toast. I looked around at the shabby little restaurant in which we sat, at the pedestrian food. The best night of his life. I understood why.

That was glory. The crew didn't become rich or powerful. But people they had never met helped them secure a modicum of justice in a strange land. God had stood next to them and faced down the oppressor, and it was glorious.

An Iraqi man, known to the newspapers only as "Mohammed," peeked through a hospital window and saw a member of the Republican Guard slap a young prisoner of war across the face. Something inside Mohammed changed sides for good in that moment. He left the hospital, found somebody to whom he could give his news: he knew where the POWs were. He could help get them out.

Mohammed returned to the hospital several times. He drew a detailed map of its entrances and exits. He noted a flat roof, upon which a helicopter could land. His discovery work took several days. And the young woman was rescued, injured but alive.

Nine of her comrades were not so lucky. Their bodies awaited identification and notification of next of kin.

Mohammed and his wife and daughter left their city under American protection. Now they are refugees. No house. Not much else. But alive. And a hero. Even if we never learn his real name.

This is glory.

Maybe glory is, in the main, a cleanup operation. Maybe the glory of God consists primarily in bringing great good out of great evil. Maybe the sorrows of life are a given, and God is that which enters into the sorrow and brings forth a new joy—not the old joy, but a new one.

The book of Job, that great study of the possible meanings of human suffering, ends in modern versions of scripture with a fairy-tale restoration of wealth and prosperity to the protagonist. He gets more land, more sheep, more cattle, even more children, more than he had before. His suffering is literally undone.

But that's a new ending. The oldest versions of the story don't end with this magical restoration. They just ended with Job coming to terms with the fact that suffering is part of life and that nobody is immune to it—"wherefore I despise myself, and repent." Let us not put too literal an emphasis on "despise" either—Job's not talking about abhorring himself really. He is merely giving up on the fraud of his own omnipotence. And on the ridiculous expectation that it's normal for there to be no heartbreak in life.

For there is always heartbreak. None of us will live an entire life without it. There is always misunderstanding, and sometimes misunderstanding grows large and malignant, and it turns into war. This is the fruit of the tree in the Garden of Eden, the contents of Pandora's Box, the end result of all the tales, in all the cultures of the world, of mischievous gods sending sin and death into the human arena. Whether there was or was not an Eden, it is certain that we do not live there now. However smart we get, however completely we master the mechanics of the physical world, we will not master sin and death. That mastery awaits another kingdom, and is the glory of it in our imaginations.

Our glory, though, is something else. Glory to God, and peace on earth. The glory of God points patiently through the smoke and stench of war to our longing for things to be other than as they are. Our capacity to imagine a different world propels some of us to seek it. Here and there, the glory breaks in like sunlight slanting through clouds.

In the reek of the ruins of the World Trade Center, restaurants that normally wanted fifteen dollars for a slice of pate wheeled tray upon tray of perfect food through the gate of St. Paul's Chapel and up onto the porch. Grandmothers and accountants, nuns, altar guild ladies and college students, Episcopalians and Baptists and atheists—all the children of God who could get there ladled soup into bowls, spooned rice onto plates and topped it with chicken tarragon, shoveled ziti and meat loaf and chicken and turkey, stacked sandwiches, opened boxes of donuts, carried coffee back and forth day and night to fill the huge urns. "I just made coffee for twelve hours straight," Helen told me, "that's all I did. They called me the Coffee Lady."

Never had we been so wounded. And never had the glory of God shone forth so clearly as it did in those days after we were hit. It didn't show in a magical restoration of what we had lost, like you read about in the spurious ending of the book of Job. We didn't get back what we lost. But we found each other. And it was glorious. For as long as we have each other, we're still here.

Maybe peace on earth is not a condition, like the condition we imagine in the Garden of Eden. Maybe it's not a seamless, endless smoothness in which nothing happens. Maybe peace is always won, always made, always searched for and found. Maybe peace can be waged, as war is waged.

And maybe there's peace on earth right now, if you know where to look. You look in the same place you find the glory of God: go where something terrible has happened and look around. Someone is working to make it better. And Someone Else is there.

4

Credo
The God We Believe In

J erry Falwell believed the WTC attack happened because God was punishing us for having gay people in our midst and neglecting to stone them to death. Or something like that, I forget exactly what it was now. Pat Robertson thought so, too. They thought so until it seemed that people might not send checks to their television ministries any more, and then they changed their minds. So who says people don't learn from experience?

My friend C—believed that God was silent and she said she no longer cared about anything.

My friend G—believed that God didn't care, either, and maybe never had.

My friend M—believed that it happened because we have been arrogant in the Middle East, but that God didn't do it.

My friend T—believed that times like this are when God does something miraculous, only you can't tell it's God until later on.

President Bush believed that God was calling us to participate in a crusade. He seemed surprised to learn that this word has unhappy associations in the Middle East.

My friend T—believed that God spared him for a purpose when he escaped from the building. Nobody who remained on his floor after the first hit survived. The only reason he survived was that he disobeyed the order to stay in his office. And he wonders if there might not be another reason.

My friend K—is not sure whether she believed that God spared her, too, or not. She was working at home that day. Dozens of colleagues died. She is still weighed down with the guilt of having survived. Knowing that this is irrational seems not to help at all.

My friend B—believes that his son died because he loved him more than he loved God and you're not supposed to do that.

The Council of Nicea believed that the Father and the Son were co-eternal, one in being, and that the Son was begotten, not made.

So there are beliefs and there are *beliefs*.

In the first days after the attack, every church was full. Nobody wanted to leave. We had prayer vigils and open discussions, communal meals. Watched the terrible day unfold over and over on television until nobody could stand it anymore. People came and ate, stayed—they didn't want to go back to apartments that suddenly seemed more vulnerable than they had before.

People in Hell's Kitchen said they wanted to talk about God. Where was God in all this? We sat at tables in the shabby parish hall: out-of-work actors, seminary students, retired people, a few of the formerly homeless, people who found themselves unable to go in to work—they worked below 14th Street, or the restaurants at which they waited tables were closed, or they were just too numb to move. Some were unnaturally jovial, like people sometimes get at a wake. People drank coffee and the crowd went through pan after pan of a catered lunch that had been dropped off with us when it couldn't be delivered to its initial destination: a luncheon meeting at the World Trade Center.

I spoke a little bit—about God, and how an adult understands God as something other than an obedient genie whose job it is to satisfy all our desires. About God being with people who suffer because God knows about human suffering first hand. Quickly, though, it was clear that the people themselves wanted to talk—some of them. Others just wanted to listen and not be alone. It was also clear that, when people asked *why*, they didn't always want to know why. No possible answer would have satisfied. And they didn't always even want—really—to talk about God at all. Not yet. They just needed to talk about what was happening: where they had been, what they were afraid of, what makes a person kill a stranger—a thousand strangers. What evil is. Suddenly, we were all impaled on our beliefs. We articulated them hurriedly to ourselves and to one another, or we did not articulate them at all. Some of us acted them out unconsciously. Everyone did it differently.

Would there be another attack? There were two dozen or more building evacuations in the first day or two after the WTC bombing. We have been on Orange Alert ever since.

"Are you all right?" I ask my daughter. "Somebody said Fifth Avenue was closed off down there."

"We're all out of the building,' she says into her cell phone, "and they made us leave the neighborhood. I'm walking up Seventh now. I'm just gonna go home."

"Do you want to go out to *home* home, out to New Jersey? You can, you know."

"No," she says, with the slightest tremble in her voice, "I don't want to leave."

"Okay," I said. Then I thought a minute. "Just walk, okay? Don't take the subway."

"Not on your life, Dude."

It's not my life I'm worried about. "Right," I said.

Somehow, you have to find a way to believe you won't be killed when you are not really sure you won't. We're not the first people to have had to do this, of course. Civilian populations in any war have to do it. Soldiers have to do it. Firefighters do, too. Actually, *everybody* has to do it, all the time: we all have to believe our lives will go on. Most of us believe this right up until the moment that they don't.

This is our central and most consistent belief. Stuff about the Father and the Son being co-eternal pales by comparison with the intensity with which we enshrine our faith in our own continuation. It is unspoken, and unacknowledged. It is also erroneous. It's not very religious. But it is central for us, nonetheless.

"Are the girls watching all this on TV?" I ask my other daughter.

"I don't want them to see it," she says. "I turned it off. When are you coming home?"

"I don't know."

"I will never leave," I told myself and everybody else after the bombing of the World Trade Center. I wanted to stay and collect food and tee shirts and socks for the firemen and rescue workers down at the site. I wanted to sit in my office with my shaken people and bring them ease. I wanted to call my children on their home phones and have them answer. I wanted to hear who had died that I didn't know about yet. I wanted to stay and see if the towers wouldn't somehow come back together, reverse the terrible shuffle of their fall to the ground and bring us all back into a world we recognized. I wanted to see if, just this once, time couldn't reverse itself, if the dead so lately alive could not somehow return to us. The irrational dream that this could happen was so strong it almost seemed reasonable. I wanted to make everything as it had been, and I acted as if I believed I could do that if I only worked hard enough.

In the lexicon of death and dying, this is known as "bargaining." The bereaved or dying person suddenly becomes a fervent churchgoer, a model husband or wife, an omnipresent volunteer. "See how good I'm being, his actions sing out to God. If you were punishing me for being bad, you can stop now."

The next stage is "anger." The one after that is "depression."

The attendance bulge lasted for a month or two. Some of the new people stayed. Most did not. Sometimes someone would stop me on the street to thank us for being there. The funeral business picked right up, and it became commonplace to see a bagpiper in full highland regalia on the streets of New York, to hear the weirdly bracing skirl of his ancient instrument as he walked along the sidewalk.

"Go to as many funerals as you can," Mayor Giuliani told us. He went to all of them.

I don't think he ever said what he believed about God in relation to the bombing. Just "go to as many funerals as you can."

New York in the autumn of 2001 was different from the council of Nicea in 325 CE. We didn't ask ourselves about just how it is that the Spirit proceeds from the Father and the Son. We really never do. If there were no creeds, and the task fell to us to write them today, we would not write them in the same way they were written in the fourth century. Much of what is included in the Nicene Creed spoke more immediately to the era in which it was formulated than to our own. All the ways of describing how it is that the Father is different from the Son, and the Spirit from both, for instance, occasioned real emotion when these ancient statements of faith were hammered out. And real conflict. Each idea about it—"God from God, Light from Light, true God from true God"—represented the views of a faction of the early church, and it was not unheard-of for them to defend their beliefs about these things with their own blood.

But today, the creed is old. We have spoken the words for centuries. They are so much a part of our experience that they have lost the power to puzzle or scandalize. We wouldn't write them as they are if we were writing them today. We would write them for ourselves.

Of course, people *do* write creeds today. There was a spate of progressive creed writing in my church in the mid-1980s, in which people scribbled earnestly away to come up with documents that affirmed their *really, really most inmost selves.* But is that what a creed does—affirm one's essential being? I think not. They're not documents about individuals, creeds. They're not really statements of faith that individual people make. They are communal documents. They don't really say, "This is who I am." They say, "This is who we are." And they don't even really do that. They say who God is. And they say that in a pretty minimal way.

The Nicene Creed doesn't say anything about humankind at all really, except that Jesus came down from heaven for us.

It says there is a resurrection, but it really doesn't say we're going to be *in* it.

It doesn't say whether we're good or bad. It's not a document about us.

Actually, it doesn't even say whether *Jesus* was good. Just that he was human and the Son of God. So that's got to be good.

It doesn't say God loves us, although it says it was "for us and for our salvation" that Christ came down from heaven. So that's love.

It doesn't say anything about ethics.

It's not a document by which one can order one's life.

If we were writing the creed today, we would probably want to include such things, because we have come to believe that we know who God is primarily from what God does in history, and to understand that to mean our *own* history. History we remember and analyze. The authors of the creeds appear not to have seen it that way; as the formal expressions of an incarnational faith, these are pretty abstract documents.

And so it is unsurprising that the historical creeds, so concerned to nail it all down and sort it all out, fail to do so for us. The nature of God is as much a mystery when you've finished saying the creed as it was before you began. "Light from Light, true God from true God, of one Being." "Proceeds from the Father and the Son." We can puzzle out some meaning from these phrases, but they are not the ones that would leap to mind if we were asked to write a statement about God. And they do not describe something we can understand. God cannot be understood by us. All we can do is worship God, and contemplate God as mystery, and serve God in our fellow creatures. Understand God? No.

Never was this clearer to me than in the months following the bombing. I travel around the country quite a bit, for retreats and sermons at other churches and dioceses. The following Monday I was in Chicago. A week or two later, I was in Virginia. Then I was in Baltimore, twice, at two different parishes. Then Minnesota. Then New Jersey. Then Pennsylvania. Then North Carolina. In every town in every part of the country, I met people who were becoming accustomed to a new God. I don't think they knew it, and they certainly didn't call it that, but they were.

The old God had protected them and the people they loved from harm. The new one didn't do that.

The old God was the comfortable companion of prosperity and complacency. Our triumphs were signs of God's favor, our wealth signs of God's blessing, endorsement of our goodness.

The new one was different. Even people who really had *not* been complacent, people who had not been self-absorbed and shallow, people who had already known life was uncertain, who had even preached about it, even those people all of a sudden came face to face with a flesh and blood experience of what it's like to be a victim, and they realized that they had always behaved as if they would *never be one*. They realized that this had been their belief—not an intellectual one, but an underlying, part-of-the-wood-work conviction. They realized that they had a tacit creed inside them, a creed that said, "I am special and God will not allow anything to harm me." Even people who would have dismissed such a proposition as ridiculous suddenly saw this in the days following the bombing, and talked about it. "I didn't know I was complacent, but now I see that I was. Extremely so."

Such people came to understand that the new God wasn't really new, and that the old God had never really existed.

We never had a special deal with God about not dying or suffering or living in fear. No creed or catechism or sermon ever said that we did. The Bible is not a story of people believing in God and living happily ever after; it is a group of treasured books about people attempting to be faithful and failing, about good people suffering for the sake of the good or for no reason at all, about one who was the Son of God doing the very same thing. No one could read it with any seriousness and come away thinking it's an easy fable about the good life. No faithful person who has ever lived has escaped death, and many of them have died much too soon.

Am I saying that it doesn't matter what you believe about God? No. It matters. It matters what we believe. Matters to us. Matters to Muslims. What we believe about God matters. But it isn't anything to kill people about.

It's something to pray about. Maybe the time for creeds is over. Maybe *membership* isn't the most important thing about us. About anyone. Maybe the "us-versus-them" sorting in which it always involves us has done us more harm than good. Maybe we should try living now, in a time of prayer instead, a time of joining ourselves to the longing of the whole world through a relationship with a living God who loves it. Loves it all. A God who comes and lives our life, dies our death.

If we were writing a creed today, perhaps we'd write something about that.

Or we might not write them at all.

We might just go to as many funerals as we could, instead.

And, in the going, we might live what we believed in a way truer than anything we could ever compose.

5

Sanctus
St. Paul's Chapel, New York City

For many years, the edge of St. Paul's churchyard was the riverbank. At the southernmost tip of the island, tugboats could come close enough to shore that the captains could call for their next orders with a bullhorn and the companies could answer out their windows in the same manner. There was no World Trade Center until the 1970s. There was no Battery Park City, which would later be erected on landfill generated by the construction of the World Trade Center. And, of course, the World Trade Center itself was nowhere in sight.

But St. Paul's Chapel was here. The oldest public building in continuous use on the island of Manhattan, it has stood five modern city blocks north of its mother, Trinity Church, since 1769. It looks like Christopher Wren's St. Martin's-in-the-Fields in London, roughly its contemporary. In comparison with Trinity's neo-Gothic heights, it is squat, dwarfed by the skyscrapers around it, dwarfed especially by the World Trade Center, which shaded its green graveyard since the early 1970s.

There is not another church in New York like St. Paul's. You enter and immediately understand the eighteenth century better than you did before you came: St. Paul's is bright pink and turquoise inside. It does not brood; mystery is not a part of its sensibility. Its windows are large and admit abundant light; the slightest of green tint colors a few panes, but there are no stained glass Bible scenes to be had here. The woodwork is bright white, from the pews to the tops of the Corinthian columns, with their stylized leaves. St. Paul's has the only wineglass pulpit left in this city, and the three feathers of the Prince of Wales still proclaim empire from the top of the pulpit canopy. The stern bronze tablets bearing the Decalogue are mitigated somewhat by voluptuous clouds, gorgeously carved from wood and painted gleaming white. Rays of gilded light—called "the glory"—stream from the center of these clouds, where the unpronounceable name of God appears in black Hebrew letters.

George Washington's box pew is still there. Ordinarily it contains his chair and his prayer book. In honor of the new president, a French painter was commissioned to render an American bald eagle for Washington's pew. Never having seen a bald eagle, he produced a startled-looking heraldic bird, plump and utterly without feathers. *A bald eagle.*

Trinity's Gothic spire and peaked windows have suffered expensively from time to time in the generations since its 1846 construction. Decades of the subway's comings and goings beneath it have shaken its delicate forms. Though the subway runs under St. Paul's too, it has not flinched. It is as sound today as it was more than two centuries ago.

When the World Trade Center shuddered and collapsed like a house of cards, little St. Paul's, right across the street, stood unharmed. One windowpane was broken—that was all. In the weird half-light of the moments after the bombing, office paper sifted down from the sky over St. Paul's churchyard: memos, printed-out emails, folders with reports still in them, torn photographs, brochures, cardboard coffee cups, newspapers—they caught in the trees that shaded the graves, drifted down to settle against the tombstones, coated with the white dust that coated the grass and coated each leaf, that coated the iron railing and all the stones, that coated the slate roof of the old church, the sidewalks and the flower beds, everything frosted with that snow of pulverized cement, office machinery and human flesh. For many years now, it has been against the law to bury anyone in the ground south of 14th street. The law doesn't mention burying a few thousand people above the ground, all at once, nor does it mention sprinkling their ashes all over the street and the buildings. But I am sure that this, too, is against the law.

Broadway is not crossable, not on your own. Police barricades are everywhere, and police officers. Sightseers have not yet begun to appear—you can't get downtown. Although the exchanges will be open within a week, it will be many more before one may travel freely in Lower Manhattan.

In a very short time, St. Paul's becomes a rescue center. St. Paul's, the Seamen's Church Institute, another Episcopal citizen of Lower Manhattan almost as old as St. Paul's, and the General Theological Seminary, which held its first classes in St. Paul's in the early years of the nineteenth century, all turn from their usual pursuits to help the workers who claw desperately through the piles of wreckage looking for someone who is still alive. It is a strange and terrible way for a new student to begin a Michaelmas term, but it is strange and terrible for everyone, and suddenly everyone has forgotten what a usual pursuit is.

The homeless men who normally live at St. Paul's cannot do so any more, not with the dust that hangs in the air and not with the church full of rescue workers twenty-four hours a day. The Seamen's Church Institute stashes them at the mariners' hotel, for now. In a month or so they will go up to St. Clement's in the theatre district for a spell, and then St. Augustine's and St. Mark's on the Lower East Side will step in and take turns. One or two of them, unnerved in a recovery too new to withstand any more chaos, melt back into homelessness. But most endure with good cheer: a bed anywhere beats no bed at all, and all of them have administered harsher treatment to themselves in their lifetimes than this serial change of addresses.

Morning Prayer is said every day at St. Paul's, though not always at the same time: much depends on when the waves of weary workers hit and what they need. There's a Mass every noonday, as well. The celebrant might be anyone—a visiting priest from Ohio, someone from down the street at Trinity, or the weary vicar himself, haggard from the continuous offering of hospitality that has saturated his days and nights since the bombing.

The garden of architectural delights that was the interior of St. Paul's is covered, now, with thousands of letters, pictures, banners, flowers from all over the world. Many are from schools and churches, all the Kaylas and Nicoles and

Maxes and Joshuas affixing their carefully-printed names or stamping their small handprints in brightly-colored paint at the end of their messages: *Thank you for saving the people—You are a hero—Thank you for helping—I'm sorry about the people you couldn't save.*

George Washington's box is now the makeshift office of a volunteer podiatrist. Our first president's prayer book and his chair have been stored away for better times. The bald eagle is also in temporary retirement. Along the walls are stations for many things: snacks, clean socks and gloves and knitted hats, sweatshirts, band aids, hand warmers, surgical masks, lip balm, cough drops, eye drops. Massage therapists whisper comfortingly to their aching clients across the back of the church. People snore on the cots along the north wall, and volunteers walk back and forth, quickly and quietly, carrying their coffee, their boxes of doughnuts. A basket contains packages of cigarettes. More than one volunteer expresses ambivalence about the smokes, but nobody has much stomach for lecturing people on the evils of lighting up right now. Another time.

I walk by a neat wreath of deep pink primroses and see that it is from a St. Clement's in England. Small world. Smaller Church. My own St. Clement's is here tonight for the 8 PM to 8 AM shift. Churches and synagogues take turns at St. Paul's, in twelve-hour shifts. My parishioners move efficiently back and forth, carrying pots of coffee and boxes of sandwiches and candy bars. They change pillow-cases on the cots that line the room; they settle blankets gently over their occupants, who sank into fast and imme-diate sleep, right in their clothes and boots. My husband and another parishioner take coffee—and, of all things, cigars—up and down Broadway to the police and soldiers guarding the perimeter of the site. One of our guys drives a truck on the nightly breakfast run, fetching stacks of catering boxes of hot scrambled eggs, mounds of sausages, piles of bacon, stacks of pancakes.

I just work the room, moving from pew to pew to say a word to each rescue worker. Many are too weary to speak, but some are talkative. Some just arrived from out of town—Los Angeles, Maryland, Michigan—and others are New Yorkers, who have been here from the first terrible day. Some are discouraged about the toll this has taken on their families. All are grim about what awaits them when they go back outside.

St. Paul's is like no other building in New York these days. The loveliness of its architecture and the sweep of its history combine with the eager service of the volunteers and the painful love of the thousands of messages to render it a holy of holies. Each day, musicians come in the afternoons to play violins, flutes, to play in string quartets, to play the piano. St. Paul's acoustics are famous in the city, especially for the light texture of baroque music. The music these musicians choose is never loud or bombastic. It is calm and quiet, simple, sometimes sad, never frantic. It is music by which to heal.

"What happened to all the boots?" I ask. The last time I was here, shelves and shelves of work boots had stood in rows on the marble floor at the back of the church. Now they're gone.

"Too many of them were walking," the young woman in charge says with a rueful smile. "Same thing with the sweat-shirts. We had people coming in here off the street and tak-

ing shopping bags full of them. You wouldn't believe it."
Then she laughs. "Well, I guess maybe you would."

Yeah. It is New York. I understand that a couple of guys
posing as rescue workers have been apprehended using the
credit cards of the dead—found them on the ground and
ran right to the stereo store. And that somebody else is sell-
ing dust from the site on the Internet. Mayor Giuliani
didn't like that last bit at all, and threatens eminently
believable woe to anyone who thinks he can sell this holy
ground. Already, thousands of urns have been procured for
those families whose sons and daughters and husbands and
wives disappeared in an instant into the cloud of dust and
fire. They can have an urn of dust from the site. Maybe a
molecule is hers. Or his. Or maybe not.

Today there was a memorial service at the site. The
mayor and the victims' families mourned together. The
families got their urns. The work stopped for an hour
during the service. So, this evening is a little lighter in St.
Paul's; the workers on duty outside haven't been working all
day, as usual. They've had a break. They're not as exhausted
as they usually are.

Strangely, though, I *am*. I tell myself that I will just
stretch out on a pew for a few minutes and get my feet up.

Today is Sunday. I began my day at 7:30 this morning,
and it is now ten o'clock at night. I am guiltily glad that
tonight is a slow night at St. Paul's, guiltily glad, also, that I
am in here rather than outside on the pile. As sleep begins
to fall softly over me, it occurs to me that I ought not to
have come. That, since the bombing, I have behaved as if I
did not have a heart condition. But I do. I have ignored my
increasing weakness and shortness of breath. I have felt

compelled to be everywhere and do everything. Sleep overtakes me just as I remember that I am not God, that only God is God. There is no God but God. I remember that this is what the Muslims say: it begins their confession of faith.

I awaken four hours later. "You were sleeping so soundly," Frances says softly as she folds a pillowcase nearby. Who has needed me while I was sleeping? I ask myself, and struggle to sit up. Frances seems to hear my question, although I have not spoken it aloud. "It's been real quiet," she says with a smile.

That's good. The other Clementines, stronger than I am, continue to carry coffee, pass out eye drops and chewing gum, serve breakfast. Some of us gather at the front of St. Paul's and begin to sing the ancient tunes of Morning Prayer together—softly, so as to be a lullaby for those who sleep and a gentle entry into the day for those who must arise.

The words of Morning Prayer were already ancient when St. Paul's was new. In 1769, this service would have been the principal one of the day, followed by a sermon of immensity unknown in churches today—an hour or more. Today, in the half light of early morning, with the candles of the night still lit, adding their reassuring wax smell to the scorched reek of the recovery site, a smell that never departs no matter how many candles are lit against it, I sing, "Lord, open our lips," and the others answer, "And our mouth shall proclaim your praise." "Show us your mercy, O lord." "And grant us your salvation." "Give peace, O Lord, in all the world." "For only in you can we live in safety."

Peace in all the world. Safety. Here, these things seem far away and long ago, in the midst of the horror outside. The weary men and women in their uniforms and dusty boots sit or lie in the pews and listen, or lie on their cots and stare at the ceiling. There are so many hearts in turmoil in this old church, so much turmoil in this old world, turmoil I cannot begin to know: the rage that makes a young person conclude that death is a prize and murder an heroic act; that war as a way of life is the only way of life there is. Old words of peace hang in the air: "Let your way be known upon earth," I sing, and the others reply, "Your saving health among all nations."

Outside, I approach three FBI officers on the northeast edge of the pile. They are standing together: this is a crime scene, after all. They are fooling around, these three: they see my hardhat with the big cross on the front, and two of them drag the third up to me and proclaim him the greatest sinner in the world. I must do something about him, they say, and everybody laughs. I play along.

"Are you really the greatest sinner in the world?"

"Nah, it's this guy right here. He's trying to pin it on me."

"Now, how am I supposed to know who's telling the truth here?"

"Whoa, you're supposed to *know*. It's your job to know. You *gotta* know. Look at him—did you ever see anybody look more guilty?"

"I don't know. You're looking good to me." Everybody laughs. "How're you guys doing out here?" It's really cold today, and we're all bundled up to our eyeballs.

"We love it out here."

"I'll bet." We all turn and look at the pile. Bulldozers crawl up and down its ramps. Cranes lift steel beams up in the air and swing them onto flatbed trucks. Pockets of foul smoke hiss from the ground. Everything in the pile is so twisted you can't even tell what anything is. Not a single object is readily identifiable.

"You been here since the beginning?"

"Yeah. Every day."

"Tired?"

"Yeah, well. . ." The man shrugs and his sentence trails off. Another officer catches his eye and he beckons him over. "Hey, you should ask this guy what he wants to do to the guys who did this."

All three of them laugh a little, this a time a grim, tight laugh, and the man in question begins to tell me what he would do to the terrorists if he were alone with them. His rage seems to be a little legendary among his friends, and they watch me to see how I will react. What he would do to the terrorists is hard to hear. I know he is telling me this because I work for God, and he wants to get a message through, a message of his terrible anger, and a hurt that has nowhere to go. He wants God to know. Where the hell *is* God, anyhow?

I do not argue with them about their vengefulness. Not now. I just listen, and after a while the man stops talking and nobody else says anything. Then I put a hand on an arm, pat a shoulder. I tell them I am praying for them every day. That is the truth. I tell that the whole city, the whole country—that everyone loves them very much and thinks about them all the time. This is also true. That God loves them and will be with them. This, too, is true.

"Blessed is the one who comes in the name of the Lord." It's part of the *benedictus*, which winds up the *sanctus* in the Mass. Even before there was such a thing as the Mass, people sang it when Jesus rode into Jerusalem on a donkey— right before they changed their minds and killed him. For us, this sentence has two meanings: the one coming in the name of God is me, every time I step out of myself to touch a life. But it is also Christ, the expected Messiah, whose coming is to make everything come out right.

At least that's what I thought the coming of Christ was about, making things right. I trudge through the white dust and back to St. Paul's. I am coming in the name of the Lord, and don't feel as if I am making anything come out right. So it must not be me. I must not really be the one. It must be Jesus.

Or maybe I really don't know what blessed means.

6

Agnus Dei
John Walker Lindh

More than anything, he reminds me of the Shroud of Turin. You know the photograph I mean: the one in which he lies on an army cot, impossibly thin, bearded, bruised and unkempt, blindfolded, his crossed hands duct-taped in front of him: *Ecce homo.* He looks dead in this photograph. But John Walker Lindh is not dead, not in that photograph and not yet.

Actually, Lindh won't die. Not now, I mean. Not by execution, anyway. In the early days after his capture, a great wave of uninformed anger fastened on him and demanded his death—his summary execution. To some, it seemed a matter of no particular importance that he even have a trial—for a moment, these seemed to include the Attorney General of the United States. We may not have Osama bin Laden, but we have the American Taliban. Lindh had actually *met* Osama bin Laden. Close enough. Hanging was too good for him.

Some months later, his lawyers ask the court to move his trial to somewhere other than Virginia, where 189 people died in the Pentagon bombing, of which, some speculate, Lindh may have had some vague inkling before its occurrence. In fact, his lawyers say, Lindh won't get a fair trial anywhere in the United States. Too much publicity, they say. They have a point: Lindh has joined the company of those who have been tried in the media, people about whom we have talked so much, for so long, that what a court decides feels completely beside the point. But this argument falls flat in court. The trial will stay in Virginia.

His surfacing into our consciousness was surreal: out of the harshness of Taliban Afghanistan comes a middle-class kid from California. California! Home of Irish Sufis, transplanted Iowan Buddhists, and Catholic priests turned EST gurus, armed millenarian cults who plant rattlesnakes in the mailboxes of their enemies. California, where our dreams are created and put up on the screen, where everyone has a beautiful body, where past life regression and *Tae Bo* mingle with cocaine addiction and vast sums of money in a cocktail too potent for the residents of other states. Of course John Walker Lindh is from California. Where else *could* he be from?

But Lindh isn't from LA. He's from Marin County.

Mmm: the Haight. SDS. Sandals. The Airplane. Psychedelics. Better still.

We thought we knew who he was. Spoiled. A kid raised without appropriate boundaries. From a **broken home,** pundits fired with the desire to protect the nuclear family were quick to point out. The problem, they said, was that he was raised with **no discipline.** That his parents let him choose what and where he would learn. That he went to an **alternative high school,** where too much emphasis is placed on independent study. For some of his life he was known as John Walker only, his mother's maiden name.

The papers will have none of that foolishness, and insist on adding "Lindh": **people should be known by their father's names,** whether they like it or not. So he is John Walker Lindh now. John seems to have come to believe that, too: he asked his name to be listed as Sulayman al-Lindh on his high school diploma. Sulayman, son of Lindh. And what was John Walker doing becoming a Muslim at sixteen anyway? What's that about? **The Catholic Church not good enough?** This is what comes of being **raised by liberals,** we read in the tabloid press. You become a **terrorist.** By the time he enrolled in a madrassah in Pakistan, near the Afghan border, he was Sulayman al-Faris. A faris was an elite Saracen warrior of medieval times. Sulayman the Warrior.

Thus, he named and re-named himself, successively honoring his mother, his father, his faith, his own religious devotion, and his ideal of military manhood. A quiet, shy, poetic boy when he left home, someone else when he returned—a soldier when he returned. A captured soldier.

John had come home for a visit, two or three years ago, after his first ten months away. He had the uncomfortable feeling every traveler has after having been away from the culture for an extended period, that feeling of not belonging here any more. Everything had changed. His parents had separated while he was gone, so he returned to find that he was in the process of joining a sad fraternity, so numerous in America, so rare in Yemen: kids of divorce. Without even having known it was in the offing. It is not hard to understand his alienation from home. It is not hard to understand, either, his being drawn to the extreme family values of radical Islamic fundamentalism. No complex choices there. No broken families. No women who rock the boat. Nobody rocking any boats. Back he went, back to Yemen. Thence to Pakistan, where he enrolled in a boys' school. Interviewed later, the master thought it strange for a grown man to be in a school with children. Finally to Afghanistan. The cause of the Taliban was close to his heart, he said. America was his birthplace, but it could no longer be his home.

My husband went overseas when he was young, too. He went to France, to work with other young people building a school in a village well known for harboring refugees during the war. They dug cisterns, rebuilt walls, went to patisseries, developed crushes and got over them, became fluent French speakers, and found friends from many other countries. They were sensitive, kind serious kids, like John Walker Lindh. This experience of independent travel was such a wonderful thing that Q—my husband—went back the next year, to do it again, this time on a bicycle. He had a wonderful time.

What kind of parents let their kid go off on his own like that? Well, lots of parents. My husband's parents, and lots of parents I know. An extended spell overseas has long been viewed by parents whose prosperity permits such a journey as a good way of broadening a young person's outlook, of building self-reliance. It bridges him between home and college. It helps someone who doesn't yet know what he wants to be in life discover it. It's been a tradition of the privileged since the eighteenth century.

And what kind of parent lets his kid become a Muslim, for God's sake? Lots of parents. Lots of parents believe in a young adult's right to find his own religious destiny. Neither of my children chose to leave the Christian tradition, but if they had, I would have kept my pain about it to myself and embraced the choice. It is not my right to force my beliefs on my children once they are of an age to form their own. The best evangelism I can offer them is the one I offer everyone else: simply presenting the truth of who I am, and who God has been for me. The rest is up to them. These adult choices are too important to be left to others—even Mom and Dad. They must be made by those who will live them.

At first, when he was captured, Lindh tried not to reveal his nationality. He did not speak. "Like a sheep that before its shearers is dumb." He tried to forestall the terrible collision of his two irreconcilable worlds, worlds that could not coexist but did, coexisted within the experience of this one young man: he was both an American and a Taliban. He was Sulayman al-Faris, soldier of Islam, and now his American countrymen, men who shared his culture and something of his upbringing, were arrayed against him. He could no longer live at home. But now home had come to find him and bring him back by force. So he did not speak. He had nothing to say.

And his accent would have given him away. He's a person who picks up accents. Some people are like that. I am. I begin very quickly to sound like whomever I'm with. I heard him speaking briefly, in an interview excerpted on the radio: he could have been a foreign student who had studied here, a person with parents from somewhere else, who grew up here. Certain words, certain consonants crisper than an American would render them, certain idiomatic American constructions forgotten and paraphrased. Not American, John Walker Lindh, not any more. But not *not*

American, either.

He was afraid of being shot if he backed out of the Taliban, his lawyers say. Not an unreasonable fear. In over his head, was John Walker Lindh. He never meant to fight Americans, his folks said—united, for now, in the face of this terrible thing that has befallen their son. This terrible thing that their son may have done. May have been about to have done. May have known. Might have guessed. "John loves America," his father told reporters. "John did not take up arms against America. He never meant to harm any American, and he never did harm any American. John is innocent of these charges." Then why didn't he notify us when he heard rumblings about an attack on America? Notify us, sound an alarm from inside the Taliban camp: *that* would have been an achievement.

His parents are certain that he was brainwashed by the Taliban. *Brainwashed*, a word we didn't have until the Korean War, a word whose creepiness I loved when I was little. *Remove the top of the skull with a saw. Remove the brain. Put it in the sink. Add soap. Scrub it clean. Put it back. Sew the top of the head back on.* John's parents know that their son longed for peace in the world, longed for spiritual peace, that he longed for it more than he longed for anything else. Their son couldn't possibly be violent. They *know* their son.

What has happened to John Walker Lindh is our worst imagining of what might happen to our children when they leave us. Our control over them, always more tentative than we have cared to admit, might completely slip away and they might become someone else. The stamp of who we raised them to be will no longer be visible in them. Another emblem will have taken its place, one we don't recognize.

And this *will* happen. Unless you keep your child in a closet throughout adolescence and young adulthood, it always happens to some degree. They're not computers. We don't program them. We are enormous influences, but we are not their only influences. And sometimes we are unwitting influences, articulating and passionately believing one thing and silently, unintentionally pointing to something else. We impale them on our own painful ambiguities. They reap our failures, however much we try to insulate them. "Family is important and will always be there for you, but we are getting a divorce." We send unintentional messages as parents, and we send them as a nation as well: "Your country is built on equality under the law, but some of your countrymen are more equal than others."

Who will my children become? I can't completely predict the answer to that, can't predict it; can't control it. It is certain that my mistakes will be part of their learning curve, and it is certain that I will make mistakes. I may read excellent books on childrearing, but my kids aren't in a book. They're right here with me, and they're off visiting friends, and they're away and at school, and they're watching TV. And my own intentions may be sterling, but intentions are not everything there is to me. I also have hidden angers, subterranean agendas from unfinished business of my own, and I cannot *not* communicate those as well, in the years we have together before they leave.

It took John Walker Lindh fifty-eight days to be seen for the first time by his attorney. He waived his right to a lawyer, but only after being told by an interrogator that there was no lawyer around anywhere. That and the duct tape did the trick, and he began to talk—you can do absolutely anything with duct tape. We heard Patty Hearst in what he said, in his embrace of a tight community that gave life prescribed and predictable meaning. We did not hear hostility toward America in anything he said.

For the most part, we have supplied our own picture of John Walker Lindh. Today, when the news came over the wire that he had pled guilty to two of the counts against him in order not to go to prison for life, the Internet lit up with calls for vengeance:

> Anyone doing the things he chose to do against
> there (sic) country should receive the death
> penalty, no questions asked, no trial, guilty.

> This a-hole should be taken to a 110 storie (sic)
> building and dropped on his f#%@ing head so
> his stupid a-hole family can feel the pain that
> 2,800 plus family members are still feeling
> today because of this traitor and his f#%@ing
> camel jockey friends.

> It's not enough. . .the bastard should have been
> tortured and killed just like all of those people
> on 9/11

> How about a crusifixtion (sic) right at Ground
> Zero!

> Hang him by the nuts, shoot him in front of the
> public with 21 guns, etc., and show the world
> we don't tolerate this kind of behavior.

And, in an intriguing and, one hopes, inadvertent, marriage of the Lindh case with the Wall Street scandals:

> Kill him hes (sic) a trader.

More and less incendiary blame traveled freely through the ether, and there was more than enough to go around—the courts, rich, permissive parents, President Bush, all Muslims everywhere, even Janet Reno and Bill Clinton returned for their share of arrows, and we haven't seen them in just *ages*.

"Youth is not absolution for treachery, and personal self-discovery is not an excuse to take up arms against your country," is what Attorney General Ashcroft said when he unveiled the charges against Lindh. But we're not at all sure that's what Lindh did. He thought he was in someone else's civil war. He didn't sign up to fight Americans. He signed up to fight the Northern Alliance, other Muslims.

"Tell me about the Spanish Civil War," I ask Q. "Did you know anybody who went over there to fight in it?"

"No," he says after thinking a bit. "Well, there was an English teacher at Andover who was there, I think. And Hemingway, of course. And Stephen Spender, and WH Auden, too." Everyone played by Humphrey Bogart in our mental movie of those times. Idealistic young Americans giving aid in someone else's war because they believed in the cause. Not unlike our friend John.

"Did you know anybody who went to Spain?" I ask Genevra. She and Q are the same age. "My friend Ted," she emails back, "he went over there and then came back and became a monk. He gave me a book when he joined the monastery. I still have it. Then he went to that leper colony—Molokai? And he never came back." Some people can't come back. Like Brother Ted. Like John Walker Lindh.

He's like Jesus, I tell Ponchitta over breakfast. Ponchitta looks unconvinced. "Well, with one important difference," she says. Jesus did good and Lindh did evil. Jesus healed people and John killed people."

They are not alike in what they did. They are not alike in themselves. But in our *use* of them, they are the same: they take sin on themselves. They stand in for others. John stands in for our shadowy enemy, and Jesus stands in for us. For Barabbas. We invent them both, supply details about them and their motivations from sources other than factual ones, create them in the image of what we need them to be. We know next to nothing about what John Walker Lindh did. We don't even know that he killed anybody.

And we know next to nothing about what Jesus did, either. Where he was and what he was doing when he was John's age, we cannot say. He comes to us when he is around thirty—we think—and we erect the immensity of his meaning upon three short years, a terrible death, and an unknowable event we call resurrection. What happened? Who was he? We assert many things about him and know very little. We may believe, but it is not given us to know.

Into his future goes John Walker Lindh. We know where he will be for the next twenty years. Parole will not be an issue. He is young and handsome: his jailers will need to protect him, or he will soon be the queen of a very ugly prom. But there are prisoners whom nobody much wants to protect, and John may be one. We shall see.

And after? After he has paid for the decisions and actions of the twentieth year of his life? His heartbroken father talked to him of Nelson Mandela, of what prison can become for one who endures it with spiritual courage and self-dedication. John Lindh is no Nelson Mandela. Only Nelson Mandela is Nelson Mandela. But John is still himself, and he still has the full stature of God's intention for him, a stature into which he can grow. That which propelled him into a radical quest for holiness can live on in him. If he will embrace it, it can reframe itself within him and sanctify even the worst days of the next two decades of captivity. He would not be the first young person to learn the hard way, though this way is very hard indeed. And God isn't finished with him yet.

7

Ite, Missa Est
New York, Autumn, 2002

Why do they call it the *Mass*, you wondered when you were little. You asked your mother. She had been told when she was little, but had forgotten. Later, you learned that *mass* means the weight of something. Matter has mass and volume. The *volume* was a dial on the radio that made it louder. So the Mass had something to do with shouting. This happened, sometimes, during the sermon: the priest would shout and wave his arms. Sometimes he would point his finger. He seemed to be looking right at you. "Is he mad at us?" you asked your mother. "Sssh," she said.

One would think that the word *Mass* would have something to do with the Eucharist itself. The central action of the Mass is, surely, the sharing of the Body and Blood of Christ. So maybe it's called the Mass because Jesus took the *weight* of our sins on his own shoulders and we remember his sacrifice by partaking of his Body and Blood?

No. This Mass has nothing to do with weight. Or with shouting.

The Latin form of our "Mass" is *missa*, an odd form of *missio*: "to send." It's the dismissal you hear at the very end of the whole service. *Ite, missa est.* Literally, "Go, you are dismissed." The Roman Catholics are a little more polite these days than in the ancient past: "The Mass is ended. Go in peace." And the Episcopalians are downright effusive: the deacon steps out and makes what amounts to a little speech, something like "Go in peace to love and serve the Lord" or "Let us go forth in the name of Christ" or "Let us go forth into the world, rejoicing in the power of the Spirit." Something really nice, but definitely telling us to leave.

So the Mass is named, not after its central act, but after its last words, *the ones that tell us to leave.* The ones that send us, not back into the past—not even into the sacred past, not even with thanksgiving—but into the future. And not into the church. Not *in. Out.* Into the world.

We must go on. And we must go out.

For a time after the attack—for quite a long time, some of us and *still,* some of us—we wanted desperately to come back *in.* To come back to church, to go back home, to stay inside, to stay in bed, to get married, to make up, to go back and get what we had abandoned. Back *in,* somewhere, anywhere. For some of us, *in* for the first time, daring to lift our eyes and behold for the first time the possibility that today is not forever. And beginning a search for something in which to find permanence.

"What are you doing on the 11th?" People began asking each other toward the end of August 2002. The networks offered those of us who could stomach it a return to our terror. Some of us couldn't watch. Some of us couldn't look away.

"Have you watched any of those television shows?" I asked Lloyd at lunch. "I haven't been able to watch a single one."

"I've watched them all," he said with a little smile and a small shake of the head. "Even the one about the architecture of the Trade Center."

"I'm not really doing very well about it, even now," I said, and he nodded.

"I read something I wrote from those days," he said, "and I thought to myself, I no longer *know* that guy. I don't know who that *is* anymore." It was my turn to nod. "I think a lot of people are only just beginning to realize what's happened to us."

"Yeah."

We skipped coffee: I had to get to the convent for my afternoon and evening appointments and Lloyd had to get back to his parish. Hours later, I was finished with my last person. 8:30: if I took a cab I would have at least a prayer of getting to the hospital before visiting hours were over. In my business, visiting hours don't really mean much anyway, but I don't look like I'm *in* my business this evening— I'm in civilian clothes, without so much as a cross at my neck to locate me even within Christendom, never mind the priesthood.

The taxi sailed through Central Park—green trees, their branches arching across the road, almost meeting in places; great rocks, old street lamps, graceful stone bridges crossing the swooping park drive—and emerged on the East Side. It's different over there. We drove past that little stand of wooden frame houses, the only intact ones left on the Upper East Side, houses that could be upstate, or in Mount

Vernon, Ohio, for that matter, two or three little Victorian sweeties nestled resolutely amid the high-rises. We passed an immense, spacious apartment complex that looked like it really should have been somewhere else, Westchester, maybe, or Des Moines, with its large garden out front (*garden?*), its horseshoe-shaped driveway (*driveway?*), its bright, wide lobby (*bright? wide?*) gleaming efficiently as we passed. "Late 70s, maybe early 80s," I said to myself as we cruised by its enormous length. Those huge horseshoes of buildings with all that space were all built then, a vast increase in New York housing stock fueled by generous tax abatements that kept them affordable until just a couple of years ago, when all the abatements expired at once and peoples' rents quadrupled and quintupled overnight.

It's not natural, though, all that space and symmetry, not for normal New Yorkers. I thought of my last New York apartment, 1840s or 50s, an apartment so charmingly out of plumb that you could place a marble at one end of the living room and it would roll to the other, picking up speed as it went, a place whose window sills tilted toward the center, making that wall look worried, like a furrowed brow. I thought of the day I walked in the front door and found the kitchen cabinet had dropped into the sink, all the dishes still stacked neatly within it. I thought of my bubble baths at night, gazing at the ceiling and marveling that the ceiling remained aloft even as the paint rippled and heaved almost before my eyes, until the day when it no longer *did* remain aloft. I thought of the Sunday morning an intruder burst through the door and asked my startled husband for sanctuary. He was a quick thinker, I'll say that for him: he knew he was in a rectory. Q looked up from *The Times* and said nothing, and the man bounded through the apartment and out the bathroom window to the roof, upsetting a bottle of shampoo in the bathtub and leaving his perfect footprint in the spilled shampoo. "He went thataway," I imagined saying to a police officer as he went off in pursuit, "Just follow the shampoo trail." But no police officer ever came. You don't call the police for stuff like that.

"My kitchen ceiling fell in the other day," Kathy said in our group meeting, and people shook their heads sympathetically in the wordless unsurprise with which New Yorkers always greet such news. I imagine the flutter of concern that would have greeted an announcement like that in the suburbs—"Oh, *no!* How *horrible!* What did you *do?*" But a New York apartment is good conditioning for life itself.

Sometimes the roof falls in, and you just have to deal with it.

I made it to the hospital a minute or two before 9 PM. How lovely to see Helen, who was thin and weak but still beautiful. We get together with friends, sort of monthly. The Geranium Girls, we call ourselves. The Geranium Girls usually meet at Helen's beautiful home in Long Island for lunch and conversation, and the others are kind enough to test drive an essay or two, read from whatever I am writing. Helen cannot be said to preside at these get-togethers, but her quiet grace centers them on the blessing of her presence. "You know, you can go out there and have lunch with the girls without me," she said. "Oh, I know," I answered, "but we all want you there. At your house." Her house with its many trees and birds singing in them, its comfortable chairs, its wonderful art, its welcoming kitchen, its welter of grandchildren's photos, its fireplace with the cat andirons whose eyes glow amber when the logs are lit.

"Me, too," she said. She wants desperately to go home.

We will meet there again, in her lovely house. I am certain of it. Its beauty sings as sweet a song to her as the eccentric songs sung by the New York apartments I have loved and loathed, sweet in a different way, perhaps, but sweet nonetheless. Every song sung in every place in this world is sweet in some way to the people who live there. Enjoy. Because, sooner or later, every roof falls in.

I felt sure I would make the 10:40 train home. But as I walked through the station, my stomach lurched: there in the concourse was a small display of rubble from the World Trade Center. Two rusted I-beams, twisted like molasses taffy; a strange orange object that had been a traffic cone; little pellets of glass, re-melted, gleaming like jewels; dusty chunks of concrete. Photographs of fallen police and firefighters. A bouquet of flowers in a vase. "Oh, no."

Sometimes the roof falls in.

Late-night travelers clustered around the display in the train station. I could not approach it. I couldn't go back to the pile, and so now the pile had come to find me. "Not tonight. It's very late. Some other time. I want to go home now."

"Be present, O merciful God, and protect us through the hours of this night," I read as the train speeded westward. An ancient prayer from Compline, the church's goodnight to the faithful for centuries. Compline tucks you in at night, puts you in mind of all the people in all the centuries throughout all the world in all its places and ages preparing for bed, sliding quietly in under the covers, feeling safe and loved by their God. Good night. Good night. Sweet dreams.

But many of the words of Compline are words about danger. "Drive far from this place all snares of the enemy." *Good night.* "So that we who are wearied by the changes and chances of this night may rest in your eternal changelessness." *Good night.* "Keep watch, dear Lord, with those who work or watch or weep this night, and give your angels charge over those who sleep." *Good night.* "Defend us from all perils and dangers of this night." *Good night.* "Be sober, be watchful. Your adversary the devil prowls around like a roaring lion, seeking someone to devour." *Good night.*

We're not over it yet. Not by a long shot. We still want to be tucked in at night. We're proud of what we were like, though, during that terrible autumn and winter, and now we know we can handle anything. We swung into action right away, even those of us who wanted nothing more than to pull the covers back up over our heads.

Everyone had always said it would take a catastrophe to make it happen, and now here was a catastrophe, and sure enough, there we all were, volunteering, giving blood, sorting clean towels and eye-drops and sweaters and God-only-knew what for the rescue workers at the site of the bombing.

It was relentless and in-your-face, our new neighborliness. Good Samaritans wouldn't take no for an answer, and I found myself accepting, with as endless a graciousness as I could muster, all kinds of things for which there was no earthly use. Laden with gauze bandages, with Teddy bears and stuffed fauna of every phylum, with cans and bottles of food from Heinz ketchup to anchovy-stuffed olives, burdened with tinfoil trays of lasagna, with chocolate chip cookies by the hundreds, we darted around the navigable streets in borrowed trucks and vans, trying mightily to get the donated bounty to the men and women who clawed through the wreckage in the service of a dying hope of finding someone still alive. And then, for months, of just finding someone.

The quantities were not to be believed. Cookies for an army, Teddy bears for the world. In short order, what New Yorkers gave was multiplied by deliveries of more of the same, from throughout the country. Some of it came to St. Clement's, undeliverable elsewhere or, in many cases, simply too much.

"What do you want to do with these bears?" Bobby asked me. We stood and surveyed the four enormous cases of stuffed animals the guys from the fire station had dropped off a couple of days before Christmas. They were inundated with fauna, far and away too many to use. Every hospital and every church and every homeless shelter in New York was awash in stuffed toys—the nation sensed that our pain had left us feeling like a motherless child, and they sent us gifts appropriate for one. It was the firefighters and police officers and their families whom they longed to shower with love, of course, but there just weren't enough of those folks to absorb the pressure of all that comfort. And of course, everyone on the force was busy down at the site.

"I guess we can give some of them to the kids whose parents come to the food pantry on Saturday. That's a couple of hundred, maybe. And some to the kids in the after-school, so that's another fifty."

Bobby nodded. "And a lot of them have little brothers and sisters."

We began to sort through the animals. Many of them had handwritten notes attached to the ribbons around their furry necks. I saved them. In the evenings, I wrote notes to the children whose addresses were laboriously printed on the tags: "The firefighters asked me to write you and tell you how much your gift meant to them. They are working at the site of the bombing, and so I am writing for them. It was kind of you to remember them and we are all very grateful." Ann Darland was laid up at home; I remembered that she has lovely handwriting and sent some of the addresses over to her, too. "You were so kind to remember them". . ."Thank you for sending the bear". . ."Thank you" . . ."Thank you."

You couldn't get into the hospitals to give blood for daysafter the attack. People stood in lines for hours. Finally the radio stations announced that no more donors would be admitted to hospitals and blood centers. The number of recipients of all that donated blood was pitiably small. Almost everyone who might have needed it was already dead.

Like everything else, donated blood has a shelf life. It came and went, and much of the blood donated in those first dark days had to be discarded. Now there is a blood shortage, as there always is at this time of year.

Even those on the wrong side of the law were stunned into an unwonted mercy: the crime rate plunged, especially violent crime. It's been low ever since.

People asked each other if it would last, our sudden kindness. Many of us pointed to examples that suggested that this energetic outpouring of insistent love was more normal than one might think, that New York frequently surprises visitors with a friendliness for which it is not famous. Look at the block associations, we said, look at the churches. But although as a rule we really are nicer than most people think we are, it is still true that we will not see the like of what happened among us in those first days in mid-September of the year 2001. Like so much about us, it was bigger than it needed to be. But it was better than we could ever have imagined.

I turn on the radio. I play it a little louder than usual, deliberately loud enough so I can't hear what's going on in the next room. Q is watching a television show about the attack on the World Trade Center. He showed me the listing about it in the paper before I left this morning. This one's about the spiritual lessons that have been learned from it. I ought to be interested in that, surely. Of course I am. Many spiritual lessons have been learned, and we continue to learn. I certainly try to learn them, and I write about them and teach about them and preach about them. I do my best.

But I can't watch the show. I can't watch any of them. I never want to see it again, not like it was that day.

Coward. Yes.

I open the mail. Someone from another state has sent me a sympathy card for the anniversary of the attack. We got lots of sympathy cards last year from people who remembered St. Clement's or had visited us. Sympathy cards! Ordinary sympathy cards—so odd it was to see them, their flowers and quiet poetic sentiments so usual in normal grief, so incongruous in this mammoth one. And touching, precisely in that incongruity. I read the little poem inside the card, see the two doves pictured on it. *A little poem. Doves.* Tears fill my throat.

Stupid.

I don't deserve sympathy. I didn't do enough. I didn't work enough. I wasn't at the site enough. I got sick and had to go to the hospital. I had to stay home. I saw the towers burning and didn't realize we'd been attacked. "I hope nobody's been hurt," I thought to myself as I stared at them. "Probably everybody got out right away. I'm sure they did."

Stupid.

I looked right at it and didn't realize what I was seeing. If I'd realized what I was seeing, it still wouldn't have made a difference. Turns out everybody involved feels like he didn't do enough. Turns out everybody involved feels a little crazy, because we stared right at it and didn't understand what was happening when it was happening right there before our eyes. Turns out many people who weren't there at all feel absurdly guilty, as if it would have made a difference if they had been. It would have made no difference.

And now not a rusty I-beam remains. They autographed the last one, settled a flag over it and carried it away. No piece of the past remains, not a piece you can see, just tiny grains of dust, ground into the dirt and into the street, but nothing to recognize.

Some of our dwellings endure, some do not. Some of our deaths are gentle, some are not. One day there will be nobody left who remembers what we cannot forget. One day people will read about our national sorrow but will no longer feel it.

This is the way history goes. Forward.

The woman who sent me the sympathy card lost a son herself. Not at the WTC—in a car crash, some years ago. Not a famous death. Not many will remember him. But she will never forget. And then she will be gone, and no one will remember.

And that's all right. That memory eventually ceases means not a thing to those who have died. They will always have been, and nothing can take that from the world or from them, memory or no. We are first tortured and then comforted by memory, and then it fades away. That is part of human life.

Our longing for memory is *not* stupid. Neither is our avoidance of it. The duration of our sorrow is as long as it is, and it cannot be shorter. And then it will fade away, as we take our places in the past. That is what the past is for. It stores our sorrows and turns them into history others can read without weeping.

Finally.